The Clash of Barbarisms

Gilbert Achcar

# The Clash of Barbarisms

## The Making of the New World Disorder

*Updated and Expanded Edition*

*Translated from the French by*
Peter Drucker

Paradigm Publishers
Boulder • London

Copyright © 2006 Paradigm Publishers

Published in the United States
Paradigm Publishers is the trade name of Birkenkamp & Company, LLC,
Dean Birkenkamp, President and Publisher.

This updated and expanded edition is published in 2006 by Saqi Books in Great Britain and is published in the United States by Paradigm Publishers, 3360 Mitchell Lane Suite E, Boulder, CO 80301 USA.

© Gilbert Achcar, 2002 and 2006
Translation © Peter Drucker, 2002 and 2006
A previous edition was published in 2002 in the United States by Monthly Review Press, New York

**Library of Congress Cataloging-in-Publication Data**

Achcar, Gilbert.
    [Choc des barbaries. English]
    The clash of barbarisms : the making of the new world disorder / Gilbert Achcar ; translated from the French by Peter Drucker. — 2nd ed.
        p. cm.
    Includes bibliographical references and index.
    ISBN-13: 978-1-59451-308-4 (hc)
    ISBN-10: 1-59451-308-2 (hc)
    ISBN-13: 978-1-59451-309-1 (pb)
    ISBN-10: 1-59451-309-0 (pb)
    1. United States—Relations—Middle East. 2. Middle East—Relations—United States. 3. September 11 Terrorist Attacks, 2001. 4. United States—Foreign relations—20th century. 5. United States—Foreign relations—2001– 6. Terrorism—Political aspects. 7. Terrorism—Saudi Arabia. 8. Petroleum industry and trade—United States. I. Title.
    E183.8.M628A2413 2006
    303.48'273056090511—dc22

                                                                    2006012652

Printed and bound in the United States of America on acid-free paper that meets the standards of the American National Standard for Permanence of Paper for Printed Library Materials.

Designed and Typeset by Straight Creek Bookmakers.

10 09 08 07 06   1 2 3 4 5

# Contents

# New York-on-the-Thames

*When I walk down the Byres Road now, I think where the bomb might fall: in the newsagent, at the bus stop, on top of the people waiting by the underground. But I am, of course, safe. The terrorists we are creating now haven't reached us yet and the Byres Road is just as I'd expect and, while I walk down it, people I have never met are dying in Iraq, are being wounded, crippled, traumatised by British forces, by our plucky lads, who will also be wounded, crippled, traumatised.*

A. L. Kennedy (23 March 2003, at the start of the invasion of Iraq)[1]

Not all tragedies repeat themselves as farces; far from it. Some of them repeat themselves as tragedies, even several times, to the point of forming macabre serials. The story of the different forms of terrorism is one such serial. International governmental terrorism (US, British, Russian, Israeli, Arab, etc) and the Islamic variant of non-governmental terrorism have now been confronting each other for almost a quarter of a century, in a series of bloody episodes whose theatre of operations has kept expanding, especially since Osama bin Laden turned against his Western allies fifteen years ago.

In its planetary guerilla war, the al-Qaʻida network has succeeded in striking the capitals or nationals of several countries taking part in the 'war on terrorism' directed by George W. Bush in Afghanistan and Iraq; after New York and Washington, it has struck in Djerba

(Tunisia, German targets), Karachi (French targets), Bali (Australian targets), as well as Istanbul, Madrid and London. It is an impressive, though not exhaustive, list. Its correspondence with the list of the main countries participating in the Afghan and Iraqi missions shows clearly that a genuinely global strategy is at work – a strategy that the heads of al-Qa'ida themselves actually lay claim to.

Yet after every attack politicians and other 'experts' are to be found to explain in learned terms that all this has nothing to do with the wars that the US and its allies are waging, and everything to do with a 'soft' version of the 'clash of civilizations': the 'clash of values'. Having run out of inspiration by 7 July 2005, the day of the London bombings, Tony Blair seemed to be parroting the remarks that George W. Bush had made after 11 September 2001:[2]

> It is through terrorism that the people that have committed this terrible act express their values, and it is right at this moment that we demonstrate ours. I think we all know what they are trying to do – they are trying to use the slaughter of innocent people to cower us, to frighten us out of doing the things that we want to do, trying to stop us going about our business as normal, as we are entitled to do, and they should not, and they must not, succeed.[3]

So the London terrorists were thus attempting to stop the British from 'going about our business as normal, as we are entitled to do'. Was Tony Blair implying by this that the occupation of Iraq falls under the heading of the 'normal' business of the British, which they 'are entitled to do'? If this were the case, it would confirm that the prime minister's thinking is, due to some disquieting sort of time warp, one century behind the times, in the context of the 'new imperialism' that has characterized the rhetoric of the British government under his leadership and rapidly found its intellectual praise singers.[4]

That is, of course, unless the 7 July attacks had 'nothing to do' with London's zealous participation in Washington's imperial expeditions;

unless those who carried out the attacks had no other intention than preventing Londoners from carrying on freely with their 'way of life'. This is the cue for the 'experts' to take the stage, never at a loss for 'authoritative' opinions that confirm what governments want to hear (which is why they're consulted in the first place). Olivier Roy, a French professor posted in London, signed an article in the *New York Times* in the aftermath of the bombings with the title: 'Why Do They Hate Us? Not Because of Iraq'.

According to 'expert' Roy, people who carry out bombings like the ones in London are not reacting to imperial expeditions as such, but rather see the expeditions 'as part of a global phenomenon of cultural domination'.[5] He makes two arguments that are supposed to prove that the al-Qa'ida network is not really interested in Iraq, Afghanistan or Palestine. His first argument is that the 11 September attacks took place before the invasions of Afghanistan and Iraq – a logic that is all the more incontrovertible inasmuch as, according to the official version, the invasions in question were reactions to the 11 September attacks. Those were even being prepared before the beginning of the 'second Intifada' in September 2000, the 'expert' adds – as if he believed that the Palestinians' oppression only began in September 2000, and that the Iraqi population had suffered nothing at the hands of the US and UK before March 2003.[6]

Roy does remember by contrast that bin Laden was induced to turn against Washington when the US deployed its troops on the soil of his country, the Saudi kingdom – a deployment that was itself the prelude to the first war that the US waged against Iraq. Roy settles this problem with a trick – 'But Mr bin Laden was by that time a veteran fighter committed to global jihad' – as if he were unaware that the 'global jihad' under bin Laden's leadership had been exclusively anti-Communist until then and had taken the Soviet occupation forces in Afghanistan as its sole target.

The second argument of our 'expert' is that there are 'virtually no Afghans, Iraqis or Palestinians among the terrorists'. This argument too is twisted, first of all because the 'Saudis' are not mentioned, while everyone knows that fifteen of the nineteen 11 September hijackers came originally from the Saudi kingdom, as does bin Laden himself and many members of his network. It would be quite difficult indeed to deny the direct relationship between their motives and Washington's tutelage over their despotic government, illustrated in the baldest possible way by the US military presence in the kingdom.

Moreover, everybody knows that Palestinians have long been practitioners of 'global terrorism'. They were even the precursors of it, before they realized that this form of action hurt their cause more than it helped, and above all before the Intifada launched in December 1987 managed to change drastically the whole framework of the Palestinian struggle. Finally, those Iraqis and Afghans who wish to strike at the US and UK have enough opportunities to do so in their own countries, on which many nationals of other countries in fact converge with the same intentions.

Admittedly, the pool in which al-Qa'ida fishes for its agents contains people who are frustrated by the exploitation and oppression that they experience under more than one heading, whether they are people living in Muslim countries subjected to Western control or immigrants in the West with roots in Muslim countries. This is a commonplace observation. But explaining everything, as Olivier Roy does, as a result of the *cultural* effects of globalization leads to obscuring the political motives of terrorism, to absolving the governments of the countries whose nationals are the victims of the 'global jihad', and to treating the phenomenon as an inevitable consequence of globalization, which we are often told on other occasions – whenever people protest against the increase in social insecurity that comes with it – is part of the natural and ineluctable course of events.[7]

The people who carried out and organized the attacks have responded themselves to the allegations of those who are trying to cover their tracks. In a video message broadcast by the al-Jazeera television network on 1 September 2005, Osama bin Laden's mentor and companion Ayman al-Zawahiri responded directly to the attempts made by Tony Blair and his official or volunteer spin doctors to deny any direct relation between the London bombings and British participation in London's imperial expeditions.

> This blessed raid, like its glorious predecessors in New York, Washington and Madrid, brought the battle to the enemy's soil after long centuries in which the enemy brought the battle to our soil and after its legions and forces have occupied our lands in Chechnya, Afghanistan, Iraq and Palestine, and after centuries in which it occupied our lands, while being secure at home ...
>
> Blair brought calamities upon his people in the heart of their capital, and he will bring more, God willing, because he continues to believe that his people are simpletons, and stubbornly insists on treating them like uncomprehending idiots. He keeps reiterating to them that what happened in London has nothing to do with the crimes he perpetrated in Palestine, Afghanistan and Iraq.
>
> Oh people of the crusader coalition, not only does Blair care little for the blood of Muslims in Iraq, Palestine, Chechnya and Afghanistan, but he also cares little for your blood, for he sends you off to the crematorium in Iraq, and exposes you to death in your own home, because of his crusade against Islam.[8]

Probably exasperated at hearing Western 'experts' claim that the al-Qa'ida network is in fact nothing more than a label that people carrying out attacks around the world claim without having any real organizational ties, al-Zawahiri attached a statement by Mohammed Sidique Khan, head of the London suicide bombers, to his own statement. Khan's statement had been recorded before the bombings, clearly in order to provide irrefutable proof of the organized character of the terrorist network's activities on a global scale. His remarks too have been heard around the world:

I'm sure by now the media has painted a suitable picture of me. This predictable propaganda machine naturally will try to put a spin on things to suit the government and to scare the masses into conforming to their power and worth-obsessed agendas ...

Your democratically elected governments continuously perpetuate atrocities against my people all over the world, and your support of them makes you directly responsible, just as I am directly responsible for protecting and avenging my Muslim brothers and sisters. Until we feel security, you will be our targets, and until you stop the bombing, gassing, imprisonment and torture of my people we will not stop this fight.[9]

To repeat: the point here is not at all to fall into the opposite extreme from the governments' propaganda machines in London and Washington, using Khan's statements in order to treat actions like those of the London bombers as wholly political, and missing the underlying social factors at work. We can agree completely with Naomi Klein, for example, when she says, 'Racism is the terrorists' greatest recruitment tool.'[10] But we can be even surer that British society at the beginning of the twenty-first century is less racist than many other contemporary Western societies, not to speak of what all Western societies were like a few decades ago. Social and cultural frustrations, whether or not they are further aggravated by a context of racial cleavages,[11] are not enough to explain the intensity of the hatred that leads those who feel it to immolate themselves in order to kill indiscriminately nationals of the country they hold responsible. Of course, ideology alone is still more inadequate as an exclusive explanation of their acts.

Producing Mohammed Sidique Khans requires, on top of social and cultural frustrations, the intense indignation elicited by the spectacle of violence perpetrated on victims whom the persons concerned identify with (victims like Palestinians, Iraqis, Chechnyans,

Afghans, etc, for the Muslim militants who join al-Qa'ida).[12] In the absence of direct experience of the violence of war exported by the West, only this spectacle is capable of sharpening the resentment felt by victims of oppression by this same West or its satellites to the point of inducing them to adopt an ideology as fearfully fanatical as bin Laden and Zawahiri's, and act accordingly. The very way in which Naomi Klein's already cited article begins confirms this, incidentally:

> Hussein Osman, one of the men alleged to have participated in London's failed bombings on July 21, recently told Italian investigators that they prepared for the attacks by watching 'films on the war in Iraq', *La Repubblica* reported. 'Especially those where women and children were being killed and exterminated by British and American soldiers ... of widows, mothers and daughters that cry.'

The lines above had already been written when I read, to my surprise, an astonishingly identical account of the causes of terrorism from the pen of none other than Zbigniew Brzezinski:

> It is a self-delusion for Americans to be told that the terrorists are motivated mainly by an abstract 'hatred of freedom' and that their acts are a reflection of a profound cultural hostility. If that were so, Stockholm or Rio de Janeiro would be as much at risk as New York.
>
> Yet in addition to New Yorkers, the principal victims of serious terrorist attacks have been Australians in Bali, Spaniards in Madrid, Israelis in Tel Aviv, Egyptians in the Sinai and Britons in London. There is an obvious political thread connecting these events: the targets are America's allies and client states in the deepening US military intervention in the Middle East.
>
> Terrorists are not born but shaped by events, experiences, impressions, hatreds, ethnic myths, historical memories,

religious fanaticism and deliberate brainwashing. They are also shaped by images of what they see on television, and especially by their feelings of outrage at what they perceive to be a brutalizing denigration of their religious kin's dignity by heavily armed foreigners.[13]

Brzezinski can indeed be very lucid – when he is not in charge himself and not in a position to influence directly an administration's decisions, as he could under the Clinton Administration through first Anthony Lake and then Madeleine Albright. He can be all the more lucid retrospectively. Thus he quite rightly criticizes, today, the invasion of Iraq, which, he writes, 'advocated by a narrow circle of decision makers for motives still not fully exposed, propagated publicly by demagogic rhetoric reliant on false assertions, has turned out to be much more costly in blood and money than anticipated.'

This is an excellent, concise characterization of George W. Bush and Tony Blair's Iraqi undertaking. The only problem with it is that Brzezinski fails to remind his readers of what he wrote immediately after the attacks of 11 September 2001. At that time, before he took on the role of a wise elder statesman, he was busy imitating Cato the Elder, calling for war on Iraq with a '*Delenda est Carthago*' chanted in concert with his Republican rival Henry Kissinger:

> The explosive character of the Middle Eastern tinderbox, and the fact that Iraq has the motive, the means, and the psychopathology to provide truly dangerous aid to the terrorist underground, cannot be ignored on the legalistic grounds that conclusive 'evidence' is lacking of Iraq's involvement in Sept. 11.[14]

This book is devoted to analysing the macabre serial of the twin terrorisms. It was originally published in French in March 2002. Since then it has been reprinted twice, and subsequently published in a French pocket edition in 2004, printed twice in English translation, then printed in India, before the publication of this newly expanded edition, which is appearing simultaneously in Italian. It has also already been translated into the following languages: Arabic, Chinese (Taiwan), Farsi, German, Japanese, Korean, Swedish and Turkish. Other translations are in progress.

This geographical reach is rare for a work and an author ignored by the big media. Together with the long life that the book has nonetheless enjoyed, and considerable warm encouragement that I have received from many readers since its publication – which I gratefully acknowledge – it leads me to believe that this little work, written in the wake of the terrible attacks on 11 September 2001, sheds some useful light on a dark world.

A new, fourth chapter, written specially for this new edition, is meant to complete the insights, by drawing a balance sheet of the expeditions that the Bush Administration and its allies have carried out since the New York and Washington attacks. In both Afghanistan and Iraq, the thesis of the 'clash of barbarisms', which is central to this work, has been corroborated in the most tragic possible way. These experiences make it possible to shed light on some new aspects of the clash and explore some of its other dimensions. The three other chapters, the introduction and conclusion have not been changed. The themes they deal with are still at the heart of current events. In addition, the time that has passed since they were written should enable new readers to note that the same questions continue to arise, on the one hand, and on the other hand to make a more confident judgement of the validity of the responses suggested here.

*18 October 2005*

# From One September 11th to Another

On 11 September 1990, George Herbert Walker Bush, the forty-first president of the United States, delivered a historic speech to Congress meeting in joint session. The Iraqi army had invaded Kuwait six weeks earlier. Four days after the invasion, the president had ordered the deployment of US forces on Saudi territory; this was the start of Operation Desert Shield. The stakes in the presidential appearance before Congress were high. George Bush saw it as his task to succeed where his predecessor Ronald Reagan, whose vice president he had been from 1981 to 1989, had failed. Despite Reagan's continual efforts and to his great regret, he had not been able to cure America's 'Vietnam syndrome'. The country had continued to be deeply marked by the paralysing trauma, acquired as it had sunk into the quagmire of the 'dirtiest' war in its history. Reagan's main foreign operation had ended in a total fiasco in this respect: the result was the addition of a 'Beirut syndrome' to the Vietnam syndrome, thanks to the first suicide attacks to directly hit the US. These attacks occurred in 1983, eighteen years before the assaults on New York and Washington. After sixty-three people were killed on 18 April in an attack on the US embassy in Beirut, an additional 242 marines, serving in the multinational force stationed in Lebanon after the 1982 Israeli invasion, perished on 23 October when the apartment building they were using as a barracks collapsed.[1]

In his autobiography, Reagan tells how 'our experience in Lebanon led to the adoption by the administration of a set of principles to guide America in the application of military force abroad.'² Caspar Weinberger, then secretary of defense, formulated the new doctrine in a famous speech in November 1984. The fifth of the six principles he laid out reads as follows: 'Before the US commits combat forces abroad, there must be some reasonable assurance we will have the support of the American people and their elected representatives in Congress ... We cannot fight a battle with the Congress at home while asking our troops to win a war overseas.'³

George H. W. Bush kept scrupulously to this principle. The first military operation carried out on the watch of this former CIA director was carefully prepared by means of an intense media campaign against former CIA agent and Panamanian dictator Manuel Noriega (who admittedly was an excellent candidate for demonization). To hammer in the message thoroughly, the operation launched during the night of 19–20 December 1989 – ten years after Soviet troops began their invasion of Afghanistan, ten months after they completed their retreat from the devastated country – was baptized 'Just Cause'. The experiment was a success for Washington, although kidnapping General Noriega cost (according to a conservative estimate) three hundred deaths, three thousand wounded and fifteen thousand displaced persons among Panamanian civilians, without counting military casualties.⁴ Nonetheless, the experiment was not decisive. In the eyes of US public opinion the operation was more like a police raid on a brutal tyrant-cum-drug trafficker than a war. It could not be considered a reliable indicator of the degree to which the Vietnam syndrome was persisting.

The invasion of Kuwait a few months later, on 2 August 1990, by Iraqi dictator Saddam Hussein's troops constituted an ideal opportunity to try to overcome US inhibitions about waging war. President Bush understood immediately the great benefit he could reap from a military action that was so legitimate in terms of international law: the first military action in the history of the United Nations to receive active or passive approval from all five permanent members of the Security Council and the great majority of the General Assembly. Bush still had to convince domestic public opinion as well, and above all Congress, whose two houses he expected to pass a resolution approving his action in the Gulf.[5] These were the high stakes of his speech on 11 September 1990.

The president resorted to two quite different kinds of arguments in his speech: 'idealist' arguments and 'realist' arguments, to use the terms consecrated by international relations theory. It was as if two speechwriters with two different sensibilities had divided up the task of drafting the contrasting passages of the president's speech. Addressing first the 'idealists', well represented among congressional Democrats, Bush launched into a grandiloquent flight of oratory on a theme that has since become famous – the 'new world order':

> We stand today at a unique and extraordinary moment. The crisis in the Persian Gulf, as grave as it is, also offers a rare opportunity to move toward an historic period of cooperation. Out of these troubled times ... a new world order can emerge: a new era – freer from the threat of terror, stronger in the pursuit of justice, and more secure in the quest for peace. An era in which the nations of the world, East and West, North and South, can prosper and live in harmony.
>
> A hundred generations have searched for this elusive path to peace, while a thousand wars raged across the span of human endeavor. Today that new world is struggling to be born. A world quite different from the one we've known. A world where the rule of law supplants the rule of the jungle. A world in which nations recognize the shared responsibility for freedom and justice. A world where the strong respect the rights of the weak.[6]

Then Bush turned to the 'realists', who rate 'the national interest' higher than any other consideration and judge that US world supremacy is part of any sound understanding of the US national interest. For their

benefit Bush explained what was at stake economically and in terms
of US hegemony:

> Vital economic interests are at risk as well. Iraq itself controls
> some 10 percent of the world's proven oil reserves. Iraq plus
> Kuwait controls twice that. An Iraq permitted to swallow
> Kuwait would have the economic and military power, as
> well as the arrogance, to intimidate and coerce its neighbors
> – neighbors who control the lion's share of the world's
> remaining oil reserves. We cannot permit a resource so vital to
> be dominated by one so ruthless. And we won't.
>
> Recent events have surely proven that there is no substitute
> for American leadership. In the face of tyranny, let no one
> doubt American credibility and reliability.[7]

While conceding that the end of the Cold War – at a moment when
Germany was about to achieve formal reunification – made it possible
to lower the US military budget from the peak reached under Reagan,
Bush added that he would nonetheless 'never accept' a military budget
that compromised 'our vital margin of safety':

> The world is still dangerous. Surely that is now clear. Stability
> is not secure. American interests are far-reaching. Inter-
> dependence has increased. The consequences of regional
> instability can be global. This is no time to risk America's
> capacity to protect her vital interests.[8]

When two such discourses, the most lyrical idealism and the most
prosaic realism, are welded together into a single discourse, one can
hardly doubt that Realpolitik has won out. Rectitude and sincerity
are 'idealist' virtues whereas deceit and hypocrisy are constituent
elements of Machiavellian *virtù*:

> [W]e see from recent experience that those princes have

accomplished most who paid little heed to keeping their promises, but who knew how craftily to manipulate the minds of men. In the end, they won out over those who tried to act honestly ... A certain prince of our time, whom it's just as well not to name, preaches nothing but peace and mutual trust, yet he is the determined enemy of both.[9]

If we reread his speech attentively, however, George H. W. Bush did not commit himself to anything in the 'idealist' part of it. He limited himself to describing what was possible in 1990 – but only *possible* – without promising to make it happen. The world was in fact 'at a unique and extraordinary moment' then, with 'a rare opportunity to move toward a historic period of cooperation'. A 'new world order' could have been the outcome of the end of the Cold War: 'a new era – freer from the threat of terror, stronger in the pursuit of justice, and more secure in the quest for peace.' It could have been an era in which 'the nations of the world, East and West, North and South, can prosper and live in harmony', while 'the rule of law supplants the rule of the jungle' and 'the strong respect the rights of the weak'.

These were remarkable words: they recognized the existence of a link between, on the one hand, a decreased 'threat of terror' and progress toward peace, and on the other hand the creation of conditions of prosperity for every single part of the world, the reign of international law, and respect by the strong for the rights of the weak.

Considered from this point of view, the events of 11 September 2001 can be legitimately interpreted by contrast as the deepest point so far in a descent into terrorism that is the corollary of the widening gap, in the course of the eleven intervening years, between reality and the conditions for global peace and justice described in Bush's speech of 11 September 1990. In a world in which inequality is increasing inexorably, inside each society as well as among nations, in which the law of the jungle and the principle of 'might makes right' reign supreme, the barbarism on one side inevitably engenders barbarism on the other. 'The threat of terror', in all its diverse forms, ends up weighing heavily on everyone.

The clash of these twin barbarisms will not usher in a world at peace. Far from cancelling each other out, they reinforce each other, in a spiral of reciprocal escalation tending toward paroxysm according to the Clausewitzian mechanism of going to extremes: '[A]s one side dictates the law to the other, there arises a sort of reciprocal action, which logically must lead to an extreme.'[10] There could be no better one-sentence description of what is commonly called 'the infernal cycle of violence', at a moment when the two clans locked in this planetary vendetta proclaim in chorus that they will not shrink from any means in their war of mutual annihilation.

# ONE

# Narcissistic Compassion and Global Spectacle

Every attempt to explain the descent into terrorism that culminated in the suicide attacks of 11 September 2001, as a consequence of the deplorable state of the world we live in, has run up against a barrage of vicious polemical artillery. In a climate of intellectual intimidation bearing a certain resemblance to the dark hours of the Cold War, the intimidation relies on two deliberate amalgams.

## Anti-Americanism and 'Values'

First, according to the censors, any systematic critique of the US government's actions is evidence of an ignominious 'anti-Americanism'. The recrudescence of the use of this term, particularly since the Kosovo war, in order to discredit criticism of Washington's policies inevitably evokes the memory of the House Committee on Un-American Activities, which became notorious not that many years ago in the run-up to McCarthyism. This 'paranoid' logic[1] always ends up devouring its own children, as it did in the past when Republican Senator Joe McCarthy went so far as to take on Republican President Dwight D. Eisenhower. In keeping with this same logic, accusations of anti-Americanism have already been levelled against Washington's most loyal allies as soon as they dared express the slightest reservation about the Bush Administration's actions.

Accordingly, following criticisms of the treatment of the prisoners transferred to the US military base at Guantánamo in Cuba, the European edition of the *Wall Street Journal* opened its columns to a certain Stephen Pollard, who explained that the European media's 'quite grotesque' commentaries showed that 'European anti-Americanism is not the exclusive preserve of the left, nor of Continentals.'[2] The European 'Left', allegedly represented by the *Guardian* and *Le Monde*, naturally hates Americans, wrote Pollard; these two dailies 'were filled with articles protesting, *Je ne suis pas americain!*' (Like Hermione in Racine's *Andromaque*, *Le Monde* could rightly complain in this case of its 'love repaid with black ingratitude'.) But the European Right and Centre are just as anti-American, Pollard continued, and include 'many of the real enemies – some might say the most vitriolic.' Besides, 'the anti-Americanism of the British establishment is as deep as that elsewhere', as the articles in the very conservative *Daily Telegraph* or those of the Thatcherite Matthew Parris in the *Times* show. All these anti-Americans had been concealing their perfidy, but the Guantánamo affair 'revealed them in their true colors'.

The second amalgam that the censors have used to intimidate the US government's critics amounts to dismissing any explanation of 11 September that mentions the existence of injustice in the world as equivalent to a justification of mass murder – as if it were inconceivable for one form of barbarism to engender another, equally reprehensible form of barbarism.

Salman Rushdie himself, though he of all people ought to be particularly allergic to anything resembling excommunication, joined the fray with all the zeal of a neophyte. (He became a New Yorker himself quite recently.) In the *Washington Post* he violently took on the 'sanctimonious moral relativism' of those who think that the United States ought to change its own conduct, accusing them of carrying out a '*bien-pensant* anti-American onslaught'. He treated them to this devastating and original moral lesson – without any sanctimony, of course: 'Terrorism is the murder of the innocent; this time, it was mass murder. To excuse such an atrocity by blaming US government policies is to deny the basic idea of all morality: that individuals are responsible for their actions.'[3] One quite simple idea did not occur to the author of the *Satanic Verses*: that without in any way 'excusing' mass terrorism, one can hold the government of the United States responsible for its own actions and the hatred that they call forth. It thus bears a share of the responsibility for what happens to its citizens when they end up being used as targets by those who commit the – unquestionably reprehensible and unjustifiable – crime of revenging themselves for oppression carried out from Washington by murdering US civilians.

In any event, hasn't the US government indirectly acknowledged its own responsibility by indemnifying the victims' families, and asking them in return to commit themselves in writing not to take any legal action against it for what happened on 11 September?[4] A banker whose father died in a 1975 attack emphasized this same point in an article in the *Wall Street Journal*: 'By creating a first-of-its-kind fund with an estimated $4.6 billion of taxpayer money (in addition to providing full federal tax amnesty for 2000 and 2001), the federal government is implicitly accepting blame for the September attacks.'[5] The author proceeded to cite many other attacks after which the government did *not* compensate the victims' families at all. This was the case, for example, with all those killed in the Oklahoma City bombing who were not federal employees: 'cafeteria workers, parents of the children killed in the day-care center, and those who died visiting the building received no federal benefits whatsoever.'[6]

In a country where everything has a price tag, we can in any case see a prosaic, monetary motive in the government's haggling with some of the 11 September victims' families. This at least supplements the political motives that led the White House to deny categorically and virulently, in the teeth of the evidence, any cause-and-effect relationship between US foreign policy and the attacks that targeted it. Thus, whereas the forty-first president, George H. W. Bush, tacitly acknowledged the link between 'the threat of terror' and injustice in the world in his speech of 11 September 1990, his son George W. Bush, the forty-third president, quickly exerted himself to rule out of court any explanation of the kind. According to presidential ukase, the crimes of 11 September 2001 could not be conceived of as a reaction to any legitimately questionable aspects of US policy, in the Middle East or anywhere else. They could only be the product of a visceral rejection of the noblest 'values' of the United States and the West. According to Bush Junior, in his speech on 20 September 2001, delivered like his father's to a joint session of Congress, the terrorists had to have acted out of hatred of democracy and freedom.

> Americans are asking, why do they hate us? They hate what we see right here in this chamber – a democratically elected government. Their leaders are self-appointed. They hate our freedoms – our freedom of religion, our freedom of speech, our freedom to vote and assemble, and disagree with each other.[7]

Addressing both the American people and their elected representatives, George W. Bush thus took them all for the kind of simpletons who could believe that the 11 September kamikazes hated the United States enough to die killing as many people as possible on its soil simply out of abhorrence for democratic institutions and civil liberties. The argument is all the more mind-boggling inasmuch as it is followed directly by the – in this case undeniable – statement that the attackers aimed at overthrowing the governments of *their own* countries: 'They want to overthrow existing governments in many Muslim countries, such as Egypt, Saudi Arabia, and Jordan.' Could Bush have thought that these three countries have democratically elected governments, too?

As if to illustrate the frankness that is the benefit of a certain degree of 'realism', Dimitri Simes, president of the Nixon Center, countered allegations of this kind with a good dose of common sense:

> Al-Qaʿida may have originated in the Wahhabi branch of radical Islam – which rejects Western civilization – but it has not attacked targets in the Western world at random. Nor has it concentrated its efforts against the most secular and permissive Western nations, which are in Europe, not North America.
>
> On the contrary, bin Laden's terrorist network has been obsessively focused on the United States. The reason is that specific US policies are unacceptable to al-Qaʿida and threaten its perceived core interests and beliefs.[8]

*Absolute and Relative Evil*

The most effective and intimidating obstacle of all to critical thought about the meaning of 11 September has, however, been the tendency to treat the event itself as something absolute and unparalleled. Is there anything that has *not* been said or written about 11 September 2001? Just one example among many, admittedly a particularly grandiloquent one: 'We will live, and our children will live on, in a history in which the explosion of the Towers is redrawing the map of the world and tracing the unreachable horizon of a terrorist twilight of humanity.'[9] In a somewhat more sober key, innumerable commentators have proffered the supposed insight that 11 September was a major historic turning point in world history comparable to the surprise attack on Pearl Harbor on 7 December 1941. The latter had been mythologized not long before the attacks in a Hollywood mega-production serving the cause, dear to George W. Bush, of a missile shield. The 'new Pearl Harbor' of 11 September, which the president declared the next day to be an act of 'war' even more than of 'terrorism', was immediately elevated to the rank of the opening shots of a new war, baptized unhesitatingly by many 'World War III'. The banner title under CNN's special broadcasts was quickly changed from 'America Under Attack' to 'America at War.'

The 1991 Gulf war in its day was already called a 'CNN war'. But the 11 September attacks undeniably marked a new peak in media globalization. No event has ever been watched by as many people as has the attack on Manhattan's Twin Towers, either live or on tape. It has been rebroadcast on television stations around the world in continuous loops and made available in the form of videos and stills on an incalculable number of websites, without even mentioning what are now called 'print media'. The corollary to this historic record is that no event has ever been as massively, pre-eminently subject to the magnifying effect of TV broadcasts on its perception – a magnifying effect which is also a deforming effect, of course. As Naomi Klein wrote in a clever reaction, '[V]iewed through the US television networks, Tuesday's [11 September] attack seemed to come less from another country than another planet.'[10]

Yet to the extent that 11 September 2001 and its aftermath are thought to be crucial events with implications for the future of humanity, critical reflection on their meaning should be considered all the more essential to the public interest. A real critical effort is therefore called for, first of all so as to dissipate the prevailing impressionism that has turned these horrible attacks into an absolute incarnation of evil. As it happens, we are not dealing with a simple metaphor. George W. Bush has invoked the metaphysical notion of 'evil' on several occasions, deliberately using the term that, as we know too well, Ronald Reagan once applied to the Soviet Union. At that time the United States was backing today's 'evil', the shock troops of Islamic fundamentalism, against yesterday's 'Evil Empire', the USSR. The United States, as is only proper, still incarnates 'good' – should it perhaps be called 'the Good Empire'?[11]

Washington is calling on the imagery of the Second World War for the third time since the end of the Cold War, after having resuscitated Hitler successively in the shape of Saddam Hussein and then of Slobodan Milošević. Continuing down the road of this playground ethics, George W. Bush has designated three of the 'rogue states' (as they are called in Washingtonese), Iraq, Iran and North Korea, along with their 'terrorist allies', as an 'Axis of Evil'. The phrase originated in his first State of the Union speech to Congress on 29 January 2002, in which the president used the term 'evil' five times. A study of all the occurrences of this word and its various derivatives in public speeches in the United States since 11 September would certainly come up with staggering results.

Evil, in its metaphysical, absolute sense, is a notion common to the fundamentalist, reactionary religious world-view that Bush and bin Laden share. To use the apt formula of the celebrated German TV presenter Ulrich Wickert, the two men share similar 'mental structures' (*Denkstrukturen*).[12] George W. Bush actually stands today at the head of the Protestant fundamentalist movement in the United States, as a recent *Washington Post* article explained:

> For the first time since religious conservatives became a
> modern political movement, the president of the United States

has become the movement's *de facto* leader – a status that even Ronald Reagan, though admired by religious conservatives, never earned. Christian publications, radio, and television shower Bush with praise, while preachers from the pulpit treat his leadership as an act of providence. A procession of religious leaders who have met with him testify to his faith, while websites encourage people to fast and pray for the president.[13]

The president's speech, after the manner of all religious discourse, has even become a topic of theological discussion. To top it off, there are even criticisms of George W. Bush's intransigence based on Christian forgiveness, which parallel moderate Islamic criticisms of the religious exhortations by the head of the al-Qa'ida network.

'The evil one': Mr Bush has regularly used this phrase to describe Osama bin Laden. Among evangelical Christians, it is an obvious reference to Satan, and appears throughout the Bible. From Matthew, in the New American Standard Bible: 'When anyone hears the word of the kingdom and does not understand it, the evil one comes and snatches away what has been sown in his heart.'

Mr Bush was raised an Episcopalian, became a Methodist after his marriage, and then in 1986 said he was recommitting his heart to Jesus Christ: a born-again experience, at least in the words of evangelicals, although the president has not used that term to describe himself. Still, evangelicals recognize the terminology of 'the evil one' as their own.

But some in the evangelical movement have questioned the phrase. 'The problem with "the evil one" is that in Christian thought, the only one who is totally, hopelessly evil is Satan', said Richard J. Mouw, the president of Fuller Theological Seminary in Pasadena, California, the largest seminary in North America for the mainstream evangelical movement. 'We don't really believe that anybody is beyond redemption until their dying breath, if they reject Christ.' Calling Mr bin

Laden 'the evil one' supernaturalizes him, Dr Mouw said. He added that saying Mr bin Laden was wanted dead or alive, as the president had done, trivializes human life.[14]

## The Uniqueness of 11 September

Criticizing the way the terrorist horror of 11 September has been treated as an absolute is all the more indispensable, since the event has been buried under a particularly dense layer of superlative epithets. It is thus necessary to put this event in proportion, situating it in the context where it belongs, without giving in to intimidating accusations that any such effort amounts to trivializing the atrocity. No one has a monopoly on moral indignation. Putting a vile act in the context of acts of the same kind does not trivialize it, still less justify it, particularly since its authors or inspirers themselves evoked this same context as their motivation, explicitly and from the beginning. Rather, to put the act in context is to reject selective indignation.

So what was so truly extraordinary about the terrorism of mass destruction that took about 3,300 lives (according to the last adjusted figure) on 11 September? On the scale of carnage for which the US government is directly responsible, and has never expressed the least regret, it was all in all a pretty ordinary massacre. Is it forbidden to mention the 200,000 civilian victims of Hiroshima and Nagasaki, on the pretext that Osama bin Laden himself has made clever use of the argument? What about the three million Indochinese civilians who were victims of US aggression – whom bin Laden has mentioned much less, by contrast, because as the good anti-Communist fighter he was for so long he had to approve of that war? Do we also need to keep silent, just because bin Laden has constantly referred to them, about the 90,000 people (40,000 children under five years old and 50,000 other civilians) who according to UN agency estimates have died each year for the last ten years from the effects of the embargo against Iraq?

Even in so prestigious a journal as Foreign Affairs, chief publication of the US foreign policy think tank the Council on Foreign

Relations, the sanctions imposed on Iraq have been called 'sanctions of mass destruction'. In an article in *Foreign Affairs* in 1999, two US professors, John Mueller and Karl Mueller, estimated that weapons of mass destruction (nuclear, chemical and biological, not counting the Nazi gas chambers) have caused 400,000 deaths over the course of history. They concluded, taking care to use the conditional tense so as to soften the impact of their statement:

> If the UN estimates of the human damage in Iraq are even roughly correct, therefore, it would appear that – in a so far futile effort to remove Saddam [Hussein] from power and a somewhat more successful effort to constrain him militarily – economic sanctions may well have been a necessary cause of the deaths of more people in Iraq than have been slain by all so-called weapons of mass destruction throughout history.[15]

In a passage that is very relevant to our own topic, the Muellers continued:

> It is interesting that this loss of human life has failed to make a great impression in the United States. Americans clearly do not blame the people of Iraq for that country's actions: even at the height of the Gulf war, 60 percent said they held the Iraqi people innocent of responsibility for Saddam's policies. Yet the massive death toll among Iraqi civilians has stirred little public protest, and hardly any notice.
>
> Some of the inattention may derive from a lack of concern about foreign lives. Although Americans are extremely sensitive to American casualties, they – like others – often seem quite insensitive to casualties suffered by those on the opposing side, whether military or civilian. Some of the inattention may also be due to the fact that, in contrast to deaths caused by terrorist bombs, those inflicted by sanctions are dispersed rather than concentrated, and statistical rather than dramatic.[16]

Here we have two fundamental factors that help explain what is unique about 11 September. The first thing that was extraordinary about the mass murder in Manhattan and Washington was that it killed Americans in the heart of US metropolises. As Noam Chomsky rightly remarked, 'The crimes of September 11 are indeed a historic turning point – but not because of the scale, rather because of the choice of target.'[17] To realize the singular impact of this particularly painful blow to 'American exceptionalism', one need only pose the questions that one commentator, remaining carefully objective, formulated on this point:

> Our feelings are unleashed, not in proportion to the gravity of the facts, but in proportion to the meaning that is assigned to them; not so much in function of the real human cost, as of our sympathy for the victims. Would the (obviously fully justified) emotions called forth by the attacks that destroyed the World Trade Center towers in New York and part of the Pentagon in September 2001 have been on such a scale if this murderous devastation had been perpetrated somewhere in the Third World? Would the images of the disasters have received quite so much attention in the media?[18]

What in fact *would* have been the reaction around the world if a mass murder of this kind had been committed in a country other than the United States – say an African country – or if the targets of the attacks had been the two giant Petrona Towers in Kuala Lumpur? We need only compare media coverage of the Twin Towers razed to the ground in Manhattan with the coverage of Grozny, Chechnya, an entire city that Russian army bombing reduced to the equivalent of 'ground zero'.

The fact that the 11 September attacks struck New York and Washington, the two capitals of 'globalization' – which means first and foremost 'Americanization', in the sense of the spread of the US socio-economic and cultural model – explains not only why Americans were so deeply shocked and moved but also why the rest of the world was to such a degree. Absolute US hegemony over the media universe of fiction and information results in a strong tendency for consumers of images the world over to identify with US citizens. This is also why people identify above all with the metropolises of the US empire, since they are familiar to TV viewers and moviegoers around the planet.

In this sense, attacks as deadly as the ones on 11 September would have generated much less attention and emotion if they had happened *anywhere* else, not just if they had hit some Third World country. The same would hold true if European or Japanese cities or even less central US cities (like Oklahoma City) had been hit. As a rule, the intensity of emotion is directly proportional to the proximity of the scene of the crime to the nerve centre of the world system and the privileged stage of global spectacle. The perpetrators of 11 September chose their targets judiciously when they picked New York and Washington.

## Globalization and Narcissistic Compassion

For obvious reasons of affinity, those who identify the most with North Americans either live in the Western world or belong to the transnational social layers that share the same way of life, characteristic above all of New York yuppies. We could call it the 'cosmopolitan bourgeois way of life', an elite, updated, globalized version of the 'American way of life' of the 1950s. Thomas Friedman, well-known *New York Times* columnist and bard of globalization/Americanization, is a prominent exponent of this way of life. In his characteristically swaggering and ingenuous style, he recounted how he spent his weekend two weeks after 11 September:[19]

> I went to the ball game Friday night, took in Dvorak's 'New World' Symphony at the Kennedy Center Saturday, took my girls out to breakfast in Washington Sunday morning, and then flew to the University of Michigan. Heck, I even went out yesterday [Monday] and bought some stock. What a great country.
>
> I wonder what Osama bin Laden did in his cave in Afghanistan yesterday?[20]

It is a safe bet that many fewer people in the world are familiar with
a schedule like Thomas Friedman's than with a life rather like bin
Laden's in his cave. Striking the same note but in a more precious
style, Peruvian writer and former presidential candidate Mario Vargas
Llosa was bent on singing the praises of the elite cosmopolitanism
of the age of globalization/Americanization by telling everyone in
the Madrid daily *El País* how exalting he always finds it to be in New
York, a city where he 'always felt [he] was at the centre of the world',
where fortunately 'the eggs Benedict and the Bloody Mary are still
delights in the brick shrine P.J. Clarke's on Third Avenue.'[21] Touched,
the *New York Times* published an abridged translation of the article.

In reality, the exceptional intensity of the emotions elicited world-
wide by the destruction of Manhattan's Twin Towers is due primarily
to what we can call 'narcissistic compassion'. It is a form of compassion
evoked much more by calamities striking 'people like us', much less
by calamities affecting people unlike us. The fate of New Yorkers (in
this case) elicits far more of it than the fate of Iraqis or Rwandans ever
could, to say nothing of Afghans.[22] Located at the very heart of the
premier metropolis of capitalist cosmopolitanism, the towers of the
World Trade Center constituted in a certain sense the totem poles
of the 'cosmopolitan bourgeois way of life', whose global adepts felt
massively at their destruction.

Only this narcissistic compassion – going beyond legitimate
compassion for any human being victimized by a barbaric act – makes
it possible to understand the formidable, absolutely exceptional
intensity of the emotions and passions that seized hold of 'public
opinion', beginning with opinion makers, in Western countries and
the metropolises of the globalized economy in the wake of the 11
September attacks.

Only this narcissistic compassion enables us to understand how
in a country like France, supposedly in the grip of virulent 'anti-
Americanism',[23] the most prestigious daily newspaper could have
gone so far as to headline its front-page editorial the day after the
attacks, 'We are all Americans'.[24] This phrase had a double meaning.
On the one hand, it expressed compassion; on the other hand, pride
in showing solidarity with the dominant country, the 'godfather' of

the family *Le Monde* is very happy to belong to (particularly at the moment when it is about to burst out in one of its rages) and that not everyone is lucky enough to belong to.[25] This is what Freud called the 'narcissistic satisfaction provided by the cultural ideal', which he explained as follows: 'No doubt one is a wretched plebeian, harassed by debts and military service; but, to make up for it, one is a Roman citizen, one has one's share in the task of ruling other nations and dictating their laws.'[26]

Admittedly, narcissistic compassion is one of the most common features in the world. It is far from restricted to the emotions felt in some countries and by some categories of people about the victims of 11 September. True, but the uniqueness of the narcissistic compassion shown by opinion makers and other 'elites' in Western metropolises is that they camouflage it as an oceanic humanism indifferent to skin colour or religion. Their pretension towers even above the former World Trade Center towers themselves. From this exalted height Western elites condescendingly summon other human groups and demand that they share the elites' own feelings, in the name of the humanism that they assume to be their monopoly. Too often their 'humanism' is nothing more than a masked expression of their own ethnocentrism.

This narcissistic compassion, added to a servile desire to show its zealous solidarity with its 'godfather', explains why the European Union decreed a European-wide day of mourning and three minutes of silence for the six thousand victims in the United States (according to the then current estimates). This same European Union did not observe a single minute of silence for the seven thousand people massacred in Srbrenica, presumably 'Europeans' all. It ended up finding a silver lining in Russia's dirty war in Chechnya. The hundreds of thousands of people massacred in Rwanda scarcely troubled it, and the tens of thousands of victims dying each year in Iraq hardly at all – restricting ourselves to examples in Europe's own geographical periphery.

This European Union, together with the United States and the other big powers, has organized a veritable conspiracy of silence around another war in its former colonial empire, which has led to a humanitarian catastrophe of genocidal proportions. The number of deaths caused directly or indirectly by the war in progress in Congo-Kinshasa since August 1998 was close to three million by spring 2001 – yes, three million people in less than three years! – according to a study carried out by a highly credible source, the International Rescue Committee, headquartered in New York.[27]

The same European Union shares responsibility with the United States and the other rich countries for failing to help populations threatened by one of the worst 'biogenocides' in history. The AIDS pandemic already affects more than 28 million people in Sub-Saharan Africa, fewer than one per thousand of whom are receiving adequate treatment. The result was 2,300,000 deaths due to AIDS in Sub-Saharan Africa during the course of the year 2001 alone, the first year of the twenty-first century – meaning more than two 11 Septembers each day!

'At current levels of intervention, the number of Africans dead of AIDS in 10 years will probably surpass the population of France.'[28] On a scale like this, failure to help the populations in danger constitutes in itself an immense crime against humanity. How is it possible not to see something deeply indecent, something deeply revolting, in the spectacle of the white world thrown into convulsions of distress over the 'six thousand' victims in the United States, while it hardly gives a thought to Black Africa in its horrible agony?[29]

## The Media and the Logic of War

The unavoidable consequence in which the attacks on Washington and New York were unique, due to the very nature of their targets, is the extraordinary media attention they received. This constitutes the second way in which they were unique. Media attention was not just the natural result of the 'concentrated', 'dramatic' character of the mass murder in Manhattan, as contrasted with the 'dispersed', 'statistical' character of the scourges that have struck Africa or the Iraqi victims of the UN-US embargo, to use expressions from the *Foreign Affairs* article cited above. Overdramatization of the 11 September attacks was also, and above all, the result of deliberate action by the media in the society of the 'world spectacle', a corollary of the world market recognized by Guy Debord.[30]

From early on, a political logic – 'the logic of war', to use a well-worn phrase – dictated this media overdramatization. It was necessary to keep imperial atrocities and global poverty under wraps, the better to highlight the 'absolute evil' that manifested itself on 11 September, along the lines that George W. Bush had laid out. Even after the historic record level of live media coverage devoted to the attacks on New York and Washington, the attacks continued to be referred to and broadcast incessantly, and will be for some time to come, so as to cover up and justify new atrocities committed by the United States and its allies in the guise of reprisals. Tony Blair reminded the media of this rule at a moment when the polls were showing a clear reduction in support for bombing Afghanistan on the part of British public opinion: 'In every part, we have justice and right on our side, and a strategy to deliver. It is important we never forget why we are doing it. Important we never forget how we felt watching the planes fly into the Twin Towers.'[31]

So that no one can *ever* forget it, the media have massively joined the 'war effort'. Even a journalist supposedly carrying on his trade as a TV critic on the French side of the Channel unashamedly hailed the 'war effort', as if echoing the British prime minister.

> What does taking part in the war effort mean for the media? Certainly not closing our eyes to the mistakes, the groping about, the glitches in the US reprisals. We must keep our eyes open. But keep them open day by day, enduringly [*sic*], without ever forgetting the original image of the September 11 aggression.[32]

Among a plethora of other examples, we can also cite these, recounted in a *Washington Post* article about the way in which inflated estimates of the number of victims of 11 September continued to be used despite substantial downward adjustments (at that point down to barely four thousand). The examples bear witness to a vengeful logic that is much more serious than the simple exaggeration of figures that the article was meant to be about:

> At a news conference on Oct. 29, a reporter asked for the 'tactical rationale' for using cluster bombs, which human rights groups say can indiscriminately kill large numbers of civilians.
>
> 'Yes, this is very simple,' replied Air Force Gen. Richard B. Myers, chairman of the Joint Chiefs of Staff. 'On September 11, we lost over 5,000 people to an intentional act. We are now prosecuting a global war on terrorism.'
>
> In cautioning correspondents not to turn reports of civilian casualties in Afghanistan into propaganda for the Taliban, CNN Chairman Walter Isaacson said: 'We must talk about how the Taliban ... have harbored the terrorists responsible for killing close to 5,000 innocent people.'[33]

The prevalent code of ethics is more flexible than ever since Western warmongers began to lay claim to 'humanitarian' concerns. According to this twisted morality it is thus highly immoral to try to put the crime of 11 September in proportion by referring to the long list of crimes committed by the US government and cited in part by those who planned the attacks. Yet by contrast it is supposed to be a moral imperative, according to the same code of ethics, to put the criminal bombing of Afghanistan in proportion by incessantly referring to the crime to which it is supposedly a response. A double standard is at work here. This is the never-ending iniquity of every form of egocentrism, whether ethnic or social.

# TWO

# Oil, Religion, Fanaticism and Frankensteins

The fact that the al-Qaʿida network and its supreme guide and financier Osama bin Laden are former US allies, whom the United States used in its ten-year-long proxy war in Afghanistan against the Soviet Union, is by now an open secret. The best description of US-al-Qaʿida relations is still a work published in 1999, two years before 11 September, which has been copiously cited or plagiarized ever since: John Cooley's *Unholy Wars: Afghanistan, America and International Terrorism*. Even then the book's cover featured a portrait of bin Laden, who only later became a legendary figure.[1]

Cooley, a TV correspondent for the ABC News network, knows the Arab countries and Islamic world well; he travelled throughout that part of the world and covered it for several decades. His book describes the inexorable chain of events that began with the Soviet invasion of Afghanistan in December 1979. Twenty years of war waged successfully against Moscow by *mujahedin* (those who wage the *jihad*) backed by Washington, its Muslim vassals, and also its French and Chinese allies, culminated in the creation of a terrorist nebula that turned its fire on the sponsors of victory. Cooley masterfully untangles the skein of this Islamic saga without missing any aspect of it. He tells the whole story: how the fighters were recruited and trained, armed and funded, as well as the political circumstances that led to their turning against the various countries involved. His last chapter, titled 'The Assault on America', concludes with a prophetic penultimate paragraph:

> From Peshawar, Islamabad and Kabul to Cairo, Khartoum, Algiers, Moscow, Central Asia, Manila, New York and finally, Nairobi and Dar es Salaam, the trail of the Afghan war veterans was long and bloodstained. Arguably, the Soviet Union of Leonid Brezhnev had, by invading Afghanistan in December 1979, doomed itself. Historians may decide that this was not the original sin, but rather the final sin, and the terminal error, of a dying Soviet Union. It gave America an opening for a crusade, conducted by Muslim mercenaries who then turned on their benefactors and employers. The world will continue to experience this blowback from the Afghanistan war of 1979–89 well into the new century.[2]

*The Sorcerer's Apprentices*

The way these Muslim mercenaries of the United States, its clients and allies have turned against their employers calls irresistibly to mind the 1857–8 'Indian Mutiny' or 'Sepoy Rebellion', when the Sepoys or *sipahi,* native troops in the British army in India, rebelled against their officers. The English press of the day was full of denunciations of the proceedings of these 'barbarous' mutineers. At this time a certain Karl Marx, resident in London, commented on the events for the New York newspaper he was a correspondent for. His tone in this account makes him sound like a precursor of Noam Chomsky. What he says is so relevant to 11 September that it is worth citing here. He begins:

> The outrages committed by the revolted Sepoys in India are indeed appalling, hideous, ineffable – such as one is prepared to meet only in wars of insurrection, of nationalities, of races, and above all of religion; in one word, such as respectable England

used to applaud when perpetrated by the Vendeans on the 'Blues,' by the Spanish guerillas on the infidel Frenchmen, by Servians on their German and Hungarian neighbors, by Croats on Viennese rebels, by Cavaignac's Garde Mobile or Bonaparte's Decembrists on the sons and daughters of proletarian France. However infamous the conduct of the Sepoys, it is only the reflex, in a concentrated form, of England's own conduct in India, not only during the epoch of the foundation of her Eastern Empire, but even during the last ten years of a long-settled rule. To characterize that rule, it suffices to say that torture formed an organic institution of its financial policy. There is something in human history like retribution; and it is a rule of historical retribution that its instrument be forged not by the offended, but by the offender himself.[3]

This 'rule of historical retribution' noted by Marx should nonetheless be supplemented by the observation that all too often those who end up footing the bill for the offender country's crimes are its oppressed citizens. The dead of 11 September were thus in the last analysis victims twice over: victims of both the kamikaze terrorists and the US government that had hatched them. Marx's purpose, however, faced with the prevailing hypocrisy in the oppressor country, was to emphasize the ultimate responsibility borne by this same country's government. The rest of his article shows this clearly. He concluded with this acerbic commentary on the indignation displayed by the foremost British newspaper of the day:

> The London *Times* overdoes its part, not only from panic. It supplies comedy with a subject even missed by Molière, the Tartuffe of Revenge ... John Bull [the British equivalent of Uncle Sam] is to be steeped in cries for revenge up to his very ears, to make him forget that his Government is responsible for the mischief hatched and the colossal dimensions it had been allowed to assume.[4]

The cries for vengeance that have filled the US media have served in the same way to hide the fact that their government is 'responsible for the mischief hatched and the colossal dimensions it had been allowed to assume.' The truth is undeniable, however: Washington and Langley (where the CIA has its headquarters) helped create and sustain a movement that then turned against them. The al-Qa'ida network constitutes the most fanatical, most violent fringe of international Islamic fundamentalism. Not long ago this fringe was engaged for ten years in a merciless combat in Afghanistan against a Soviet army that itself gave no quarter.

Whether visionary fanatics or (re-)converted delinquents,[5] many members of al-Qa'ida – as soon as they were demobilized in Afghanistan at the end of the war against the Soviets and their allies – turned their guns against the governments of the countries they came from: Algeria, 'Saudi' Arabia,[6] China, Egypt, Uzbekistan, the Philippines, Russia, Tadzhikistan, Chechnya, Tunisia, etc. In each of these countries they joined or helped found local networks devoted to armed struggle and to the assassination of civilians for political or ideological ends that is commonly called 'terrorism'. During the Afghan war the networks of armed Islamic fanaticism had been funded by both state and private sources – first and foremost by the US government and its Saudi protégés, but also by private donors from the Saudi kingdom and other oil states and Muslim countries, who were urged on by their countries' governments and religious authorities. After the networks' anti-communist mission ended, however, their sources of state funding dried up.

They were carrying on their battle, but this time against governments allied with the West. They nonetheless managed to keep some of the private financing they had been receiving before, thanks to either the donors' sympathy for their cause or intimidation – or even misappropriation of charitable gifts. They used tricks to transfer funds covertly and launder dirty money resulting from the drug trade and other traffics – all methods that the CIA had used long before they did, that the CIA had in fact trained them in during the war against the Soviet Union.

The Pakistani military dictatorship tried, in alliance with the Saudi monarchy, sometimes officially and sometimes unofficially, to keep the Afghan blaze under control and limit the export of terrorists that it had brought forth, as the Lebanese conflagration had earlier. Islamabad tried to achieve this end by supporting a march on Kabul by fundamentalists – the Taliban – trained as fanatics in Afghan refugee camps in Pakistan, with the help of Riyadh. The Taliban's conquest of most of Afghanistan in 1994–6 occurred with Washington's blessing, given out of considerations that had as much to do with politics as with oil. Yet soon the Taliban in their turn proved to be out of control.

All these facts are now well known. John Cooley's book had already laid them out in great detail. They are all reminiscent of the allegorical figure described by Goethe in his ballad 'The Sorcerer's Apprentice', or by Mary (Wollstonecraft) Shelley in her comparable novel *Frankenstein, or The Modern Prometheus*. In both tales, the creature escapes its creator's control and turns against him. Yet in another way the demiurge in Washington is unlike those two guileless characters, 'The Sorcerer's Apprentice' and Victor Frankenstein (who, contrary to the prevailing confusion, was not the monster but only the man who put it together out of bits and pieces of corpses): it is itself monstrous. This contemporary Frankenstein knew quite well that by assembling the elements produced by the decomposition of various Muslim societies, it was creating and feeding a monster. It did this with a definite purpose: the monster was meant to do the dirty work that the creator itself was unable to carry out. Nevertheless, the demon still ultimately turned against the demiurge. In the process, on 11 September 2001, the monster killed thousands of men and women who were in no way responsible for the US government's activities.

### An Islamic Texas

The al-Qa'ida network is in any event only one of the maddened avatars of Islamic fundamentalism, a political current that Washington has sustained for more than half a century. By an irony of history, most of the 11 September hijackers – fifteen out of nineteen – were 'Saudi' subjects. So was their supreme guide bin Laden (though bin Laden was stripped of his nationality in 1994). The fact is, however, that the Saudi kingdom is one of the United States' longest-standing international partners. Born of the alliance forged in the eighteenth century between Muhammad bin Abdel-Wahhab's ultra-puritan Hanbalite[7] Islamic preaching fraternity and Muhammad bin Saud's tribal chiefdom, the kingdom was established on territory that Abdel-Aziz bin Abdel-Rahman, better known as Ibn Saud, conquered during the early decades of the twentieth century. It was proclaimed in 1932 under the name Saudi Arab Kingdom, from the name of the Âl Saud dynasty (the House of Saud) derived from its founding ancestor's given name.

At about this time the discovery of oil in the Arab Persian Gulf region and the growing economic importance of this basic energy resource had given rise to considerable rivalry between British interests, which had established themselves in the region many years earlier, and the Johnny-come-lately United States. The vast desert area of the Arabian peninsula, which had long been neglected by the foreign powers dominating the region, began to arouse imperialist cupidity. The first concession contract granted by Ibn Saud, in 1933, landed in the hands of the US oil company Standard Oil of California (Socal, the precursor of Chevron). Socal had taken a certain risk in outbidding its largely British rivals, since the kingdom's oil wealth was still only hypothetical.[8] That same year, 1933, the US government established diplomatic relations with the Saudi kingdom. It was the beginning of an alliance that would last into our own times.

During the Second World War the kingdom's strategic importance in US eyes increased considerably, thanks to a leap in world petroleum consumption combined with the discovery of the vast oil resources lying under the Saudi kingdom's surface. As early as 1943 the wartime US government showed its strategic interest in the kingdom by taking the decision to build a major air base at Dhahran,[9] near wells operated by Aramco (Arabian-American Oil Company). Aramco, a joint venture between Socal and Texaco, would quickly become a state within the Saudi state. From then on the US commitment to protect the Saudi realm has been reaffirmed, and tested in practice, several times:

> Soviet expansionism – as it was, and as it might be – brought the Middle East to center stage. To the United States, the oil resources of the region constituted an interest no less vital, in its own way, than the independence of western Europe; and the Middle Eastern oil fields had to be preserved and protected on the western side of the Iron Curtain to assure the economic survival of the entire Western world.
>
> Saudi Arabia became the dominant focus of American policymakers. Here was, said one American official in 1948, 'what is probably the richest economic prize in the world in the field of foreign investment.'[10]

If Ibn Saud for his part chose to privilege an alliance with Washington, this was not due only to the good reasons he had to be suspicious of the British – he had been fighting against the main Arab ally of the British, the Hashemite dynasty, who were the Âl Sauds' rivals and in power at the time in Iraq and Transjordan. He also felt a certain 'elective affinity' with the United States. An episode recounted in Daniel Yergin's voluminous history of the oil industry shows this clearly. Ibn Saud had two contrasting meetings within three days in 1945, one with Franklin D. Roosevelt (on his way home from Yalta) and one with Winston Churchill. While the US president took pains to respect his Saudi partner's religious beliefs, the British prime minister insisted on drinking alcohol and smoking his cigar in the presence of his austere royal host.[11]

This anecdote is symptomatic of an important difference between the United Kingdom and United States. The Puritans, themselves an ultra-fundamentalist Presbyterian sect, had certain points in common with the Wahhabites. Persecuted by the English monarchy in the sixteenth and seventeenth centuries, they were one of the original sources of European colonization in North America, as the famous episode of the Mayflower (1620) symbolically attests. The contribution of religious fundamentalist currents to US history is well known. Even today in many states of the Union the evolutionary biology founded by Darwin is treated with abhorrence; many people continue to wage war on it in the name of 'scientific creationism'. The same people seek to impose compulsory prayer in schools.

Religious tolerance, not secularism, is at the heart of the US institutional edifice. Sessions of Congress open with prayers; trust in God is proclaimed even on the national currency, the dollar. Several big names of the US intelligentsia recently boasted in a collective manifesto, 'We have a secular state – our government officials are not simultaneously religious officials – but we are by far the Western world's most religious society.'[12]

As a job requirement, as it were, the occupants of the White House are consequently predisposed to show 'understanding' toward their Saudi protégés and clients' Islamic fundamentalism. They are all the more disposed to make allowances because the kingdom's importance for Washington has continued to grow. For many years the primary foreign oil supplier for the United States, the Saudi kingdom is still in the race for first place with Canada and Venezuela. Yet its trade with its protector is almost in balance, thanks notably to its vast arms imports and its contracts with US construction firms, which have grown impressively since the 1974 oil boom. With the world's ninth-largest military budget today, the Saudi kingdom has been the world's largest arms importer and the main purchaser of US arms in recent years. It has thus put a seal on its 'complementarity' with its protector, which is the world's largest arms exporter.

The kingdom's importance to Washington was summed up very well in a recent report by the US human rights organization Human Rights Watch:

For the United States, Saudi Arabia, as the world's largest oil exporter, is a vital ally. Over half of the kingdom's crude oil exports, and the majority of its refined petroleum exports, go to Asia, while the US gets 17 percent of its crude oil imports from Saudi Arabia. US civilian and military merchandise exports to the country in 2000 totaled $6.23 billion, according to the US embassy in Riyadh, and investments in the country by US-based multinationals are around $5 billion. Saudi investments in the US total nearly half a trillion dollars, mainly in stocks and bonds, bank deposits, and real estate, according to US officials. Saudi Arabia is by far the top customer for US arms exports among developing countries, taking deliveries worth more than $28 billion in the 1993–2000 period, according to the latest annual report on arms transfers from the Congressional Research Service.[13]

Nor is the US interest in the kingdom's oil limited to the direct US trading relationship. The key role that 'Saudi' Arabia plays on the world oil market, as the country with the biggest margin of variation in its oil exports, is absolutely essential for Washington. The kingdom has often intervened in this market in order to provide for the needs of the US economy. It has a direct interest in the US economy's performance and the dollar's strength in any event, given that most of its enormous foreign assets are invested in the United States.[14]

The Saudi kingdom's military expenditure is a necessary counterpart of its oil and financial relationship with its tutelary power. It is a 'protected kingdom' in the historic sense of the term. Saudi military spending is in large part the kingdom's direct contribution to the costs of its military protection by the United States. According to Zbigniew Brzezinski's apt formula, the relationship is one of 'asymmetrical interdependence':

> We need their oil and therefore we have to make sure that they are friendly and therefore we are engaged in protecting

their security. They, at the same time, are almost completely dependent on us for their security in a region in which they're very vulnerable and very rich. So there is a kind of a curious, though asymmetrical, interdependence here.[15]

Only about 50 percent of the amounts spent on the basis of the military contracts that the kingdom signed with the United States during the second half of the twentieth century went toward the actual material supplied; the rest was spent on maintenance (not counting spare parts), training and construction.[16] The kingdom's 1981 contract for the acquisition of five Awacs radar planes is an enlightening example; as a journalist for the *Washington Post* discovered, the funds committed amounted to ten times the selling price of the airplanes ($5.5 billion as opposed to $550 million).[17] These arms deals actually served to finance construction of military installations as well as pre-positioning of military equipment put at the disposal of the US armed forces. This explains the ease and rapidity with which the United States was able to deploy a formidable armada on Saudi territory and make it operational in 1990.

The Iranian revolution of 1979 had set off alarms in both Riyadh and Washington. The Carter Administration subsequently decided to set up a rapid reaction force that would be ready to intervene in the Gulf region. The necessary infrastructure for this rapid intervention was built in the Saudi kingdom itself – as this same Brzezinski, then Jimmy Carter's national security adviser, explained:

We therefore developed the proposal for the rapid deployment force and for arrangements for the pre-positioning of some facilities, equipment, and logistical facilities in the area. We didn't ask for bases, but we asked for access which, in effect, operationally, wasn't all that different.[18]

The Saudi kingdom then threw itself in the 1980s into a frenzy of military spending, aided by the sharp increase in oil prices in the wake of the Iranian revolution and the start of the Iran-Iraq war. This frenzy was the Middle Eastern pendant to the military extravagance of the Reagan Administration. Lawrence Korb, then a member of the administration as deputy secretary of defence under Caspar Weinberger, gave a good summary of the real function of Saudi spending in this period:

> What the Saudis allowed the United States to do over in that part of the world was to set up a *de facto* infrastructure by purchasing airfields, by purchasing very modern ports, by purchasing a lot of American equipment, theoretically to support their forces, by buying a lot of American equipment that would use the same type of facilities that our forces needed. So, in effect, we had a replica of US airfields and ports over in that part of the world paid for by the Saudis to be used by the United States when and if we had to go over there.[19]

When US forces did 'have to go over there' for the Gulf war in 1990–91, the Saudi kingdom spent a total of $55 billion, much of it to cover the costs of the US troops on its soil, and $17 billion donated directly to the United States as a contribution to financing the US war effort. The kingdom has incidentally been contributing to financing the US budget for many years through its massive purchases of US Treasury bonds. This was particularly the case during the years of record budget deficits due to military spending under Reagan. In short, all things considered, the Saudi kingdom can legitimately be considered a fifty-first state of the United States of America,[20] a sort of Islamic Texas.

## Propagating Islamic Fundamentalism

This US state *sui generis* was based from the time it was created on a separation of powers, in the continuity of the founding pact made in the eighteenth century between Sheik Muhammad bin Saud and the preacher Muhammad bin Abdel-Wahhab. The House of Saud reserved control of the kingdom's economy, defence and foreign policy for itself, while it granted the Wahhabite religious order the final say on religious affairs, education and regulation of daily life. This separation of powers has not always functioned harmoniously, however. When the Wahhabite *Ikhwan* ('Brothers') still constituted an armed force, in the days when Abdel-Aziz Ibn Saud led them personally in a war of tribal conquest, they went so far as to challenge the man who had proclaimed himself king in 1926, because he had not respected their absolute rejection of any modern invention (not unlike the Anabaptist Amish sect in the United States). Ibn Saud had to tame them by using various means, including force.

The rise of republican, progressive Arab nationalism in the 1950s – under the charismatic leadership of Gamal Abdel-Nasser, who had overthrown the Egyptian monarchy in 1952 – and its alliance with the Soviet Union from the mid-1950s halted the drift toward divorce between the House of Saud and the Wahhabite establishment. From then on the Wahhabites were seen as the Saudi monarchy's best social and ideological bulwark against Arab anti-imperialism, which it accused of supporting 'atheistic communism'. The kingdom's godfathers in the United States saw the situation in the same way and encouraged their Saudi protégés to rely on the Wahhabites.

Islamic fundamentalism – most of whose varieties allied under Wahhabite tutelage – subsequently became the main ideological tool of the anti-communist and anti-nationalist struggle in the Islamic world, orchestrated by Washington in alliance with Riyadh. This same linkage was at the source of Islamic fundamentalism in its contemporary political version, in the form of the society of the Muslim Brotherhood (*al-Ikhwan al-muslimun*), born in Egypt in the late 1920s. Wahhabite expansionism fascinated Rashid Rida, the Brotherhoods' ideological inspirer and an upholder of the most reactionary form of the *salafiyya* (doctrine of the return to the original Islam of its founding epoch), and Rida cultivated ties with Ibn Saud.[21]

The Saudi kingdom's status as protector of Islam's holy sites, particularly Mecca, implied from the beginning that its Islamic policies would have an international scope. Every practising Muslim is supposed to visit Mecca at least once in his or her life; this pilgrimage is one of the five 'pillars' of the Muslim religion. The fact that the fanatical, minority Wahhabite sect controlled the Hijaz, the most sacred province of all in Muslims' eyes, was a source of problems. In order to lay people's fears to rest and build a consensus around Saudi management of the holy sites, Ibn Saud organized an Islamic Congress in Mecca as early as 1926. The congress brought together Muslim religious organizations from various countries, where Muslims constituted majorities as well as minorities.

The 'Arab cold war'[22] and the violent opposition between the US-backed Saudi monarchy and Soviet-allied Nasserite Egypt, then at its most radical, reached their height in 1962. That was the year that the Egyptian National Charter proclaimed 'socialism' combined with Arab nationalism and anti-imperialism. That same year the Saudi kingdom and Wahhabite establishment founded the Muslim World League, which brought together various Muslim institutions and organizations from many countries on the model of the 1926 Islamic Congress. The League became the crucible for an alliance between the Wahhabites and the Muslim Brotherhood, many of whose leaders had taken refuge in the Saudi kingdom after fleeing from countries where nationalists had taken power. The League contributed, with CIA backing, to propagating reactionary Islam as an adversary of populist nationalism.

Israel's victory in the June 1967 Six-Day War was a deadly blow to Nasserism, compounded by Nasser's death in 1970. Combined with the sudden spurt in oil prices following the fourth Arab-Israeli war in October 1973, it considerably strengthened the Saudi kingdom's influence in the Arab and Muslim worlds. But the Iranian 'Islamic revolution' of 1979 faced the Saudi rulers with an unexpected ideological challenge: anti-Western radicalism, which would henceforth combine with Islamic fundamentalism of the Khomeini is happened at the very moment when a panicky Soviet pushing out for the first time beyond its own post-1945 imperial domain in order to invade a Muslim country, Afghanistan. In these unprecedented conditions, the Saudi-Wahhabite ideological enterprise threw itself into a more-radical-than-thou contest with Khomeini-inspired Islamic fundamentalism. The Saudis counterposed their predominantly anti-communist fanaticism to the Khomeini pattern of predominantly anti-Western fanaticism. As is often the case with such rivalries, each form of fanaticism bled into and coloured the other. The Muslim-Soviet war in Afghanistan was the main arena in which they competed, with the CIA's continued backing.

The United States is thus directly responsible for the resurgence of anti-Western Islamic fundamentalism. Over the past thirty years this resurgence has flourished in two successive waves. The Iranian revolution marked the climax of the first wave, in the 1970s; 11 September and the shock wave it sent out were the peak of the second wave, dating back to the 1990s. The United States is in fact doubly responsible for them. Not only did it contribute directly to propagating Islamic fundamentalism, but by helping to defeat and crush the Left and progressive nationalism throughout the Islamic world, it freed up the space for political Islam as the only ideological and organizational expression of popular resentment. Popular resentment, like nature, abhors a vacuum. The resurgence of Islamic fundamentalism is not the culturally inevitable form of radicalization in Muslim countries; until recently most people in Muslim countries spurned the ideology. It won out only by default, after its competition was eliminated by their common adversary.

Several different factors – the world-wide loss of ideological credibility of socialist values, due to the collapse of the Stalinist system; the specific failure or marginality of all currents of the Left in the Muslim world; Islamic fundamentalism's smooth slide down a chute well oiled by Washington and Riyadh; a context of economic crisis and growing social insecurity against a backdrop of neoliberal deregulation on a world scale, and all of this aggravated by the affronts experienced daily by Muslim peoples who identify with the Palestinians or Iraqis – have converged to produce a highly explosive mixture in the form of the most virulent Islamic antagonism to the West. In these conditions 'the *opium* of the people', which the young Marx had conceived of as a narcotic with a sedative effect, religion as the 'halo' over this 'vale of tears', can become a powerful stimulant and the 'sigh of the oppressed creature' can turn into a scream of rage.[23] Plebeian social layers as well as the middle classes are all the more enraged inasmuch as they have suffered a sharp drop in status and lost their cultural and ideological bearings. They form a natural breeding ground for this manifestation of social, national and cultural hatred.

Those who thought they could use 'the opium of the people' against 'Communism' – much as the CIA used opium itself against the Soviet troops in Afghanistan – have ended up seeing the boomerang slam back onto their own home ground. In this respect the most telling example of the sorcerer's apprentice was for a time Anwar al-Sadat. Spurred on politically and financially by the Saudi kingdom and its patrons in Washington, Sadat used Islamic fundamentalist currents against the Egyptian Left and Nasserites only to end up assassinated himself by enraged fundamentalists. Other illustrations of the same phenomenon, including Israel's complicity in the rise of Hamas, are too numerous to mention here. The example of Sadat has now been surpassed by 11 September, the supreme illustration of the same allegory of a phenomenon turning against its creator.

## Interpretations of Islamic Fundamentalism

The crest of the first wave of the resurgence of Islamic fundamentalism gave rise to an extensive discussion, which still continues today, about how to analyse the phenomenon. I myself developed a Marxist analysis more than twenty years ago, which inspired the passages above. It seems to me to have stood the test of time. I therefore take the liberty of citing some long extracts from the article here, despite its slight aura of jargon due to being written for a politically engaged forum. The analysis drew on an intuition expressed in Marx and Engels's *Communist Manifesto*:

> The lower middle class, the small manufacturer, the shopkeeper, the artisan, the peasant, all these fight against the bourgeoisie, to save from extinction their existence as fractions of the middle class. They are therefore not revolutionary, but conservative. Nay more, they are reactionary, for they try to roll back the wheel of history.[24]

Beginning with a definition of Islamic fundamentalism and emphasizing the diversity of its forms and currents, the article continued:

> Petty bourgeois Islamic reaction finds its ideologues and leading elements among the 'traditional intellectuals' of Muslim societies, ulemas and the like, as well as among the lower echelons of the bourgeoisie's 'organic intellectuals,' those coming from the petty bourgeoisie and condemned to stay there: teachers and office workers in particular. In a period of ascendancy Islamic fundamentalism recruits widely at universities and other institutions that produce 'intellectuals,' where they are still more conditioned by their social origins than by a hypothetical and often doubtful future.
>
> In countries where Islamic fundamentalist reaction has been able to become a mass movement and where it now has the wind in its sails, the labor force includes a relatively high proportion of middle classes, according to the *Communist Manifesto* definition: manufacturers, shopkeepers, artisans and peasants. Nevertheless, any outbreak of Islamic fundamentalism mobilizes not only a larger or smaller layer of these middle classes, but also layers of other classes newly spawned by the middle classes under the impact of capitalist primitive accumulation and impoverishment.

Thus parts of the proletariat whose proletarianization is very recent, and above all parts of the sub-proletariat that capitalism has dragged down from their former petty bourgeois level, are particularly receptive to fundamentalist agitation and susceptible to being caught up in it.

This is Islamic fundamentalism's social base, its mass base. *But this base is not the natural preserve of religious reaction*, the way that the bourgeoisie relates to its own program. *Whatever the strength of religious feeling among the masses, even if the religion in question is Islam, there is a qualitative leap from sharing this feeling to seeing religion as an earthly utopia.* In order for the opiate of the masses to become an effective stimulant once more in this age of automation, the peoples must truly have no other choice left but to throw themselves on God's mercy. The least one can say about Islam is that its immediate relevance is not obvious! In fact, Islamic fundamentalism poses more problems than it solves ... In other words, the most orthodox Muslim fundamentalist is incapable of responding to the problems posed by modern society with exegetical contortions alone, unless the contortions become totally arbitrary and therefore a source of endless disagreements among the exegetes. There are thus as many interpretations of Islam as there are interpreters. The core of the Islamic religion, which all Muslims agree on, in no way satisfies the pressing material needs of the petty bourgeois, quite apart from whether it can satisfy their spiritual needs. *Islamic fundamentalism in itself is in no way the most appropriate program for satisfying the aspirations of the social layers that it appeals to.*

... *The middle classes are first and foremost the social base of the democratic revolution and the national struggle.* In backward, dependent societies such as Muslim societies the middle classes still play this role as long as the tasks of the national and democratic revolution are still more or less uncompleted and on the agenda. They are the most ardent fans of any bourgeois leadership (and even more of any petty bourgeois leadership) that champions these tasks. The middle classes are the social base par excellence of the Bonapartism of the ascendant bourgeoisie; they are in fact the social base of all bourgeois Bonapartism. So the only time when large sections of the middle classes strike off on their own and seek other paths is when bourgeois or petty bourgeois leaderships that have taken on national and democratic tasks run up against their own limits and lose their credibility.

Of course, as long as capitalism on the rise seems to open up prospects of upward social mobility for the middle classes, as long as their conditions of existence are improving, they do not question the established order. Even when depoliticized or unenthused, they normally play the role of 'silent majority' in the bourgeois order. But if ever the capitalist evolution of society weighs on them with all its force – the weight of national and/ or international competition, inflation and debt – then the middle classes become a formidable reservoir of opposition to the powers that be. Then they are free of any bourgeois control, and all the more formidable because the violence and rage of the petty bourgeois in distress are unparalleled.[25]

The point of reprinting this more than twenty-year-old analysis here is that this allows us to compare it in a useful way with other, much more recent diagnoses and prognoses of the phenomenon of Islamic fundamentalism. The central contention of the Marxist analysis cited above is that radical, anti-Western Islamic fundamentalism is a distorted, reactionary expression of the middle classes' and plebeian layers' resentment against distorted capitalist development and Western domination, often exacerbated by a despotic local state. This expression has prevailed following the failure or elimination of modernist expressions of this same resentment, whether nationalist, anti-imperialist and populist; anti-capitalist and socialist; or a combination of these dimensions.

The logical corollary of this thesis is that Islamic fundamentalism could only be displaced from centre stage on the oppositional scene in one of two ways. One possibility would be a takeoff of capitalist development in the regions where Islamic fundamentalism has been spreading, through a sustained 'virtuous circle' of growth in a form that would benefit the population as a whole. This kind of growth is habitually referred to as an 'economic miracle'; in this case the term would be entirely justified. The only other possibility is for new progressive or revolutionary forms of anti-imperialist, more or less anti-capitalist, struggle to prevail once more as the majoritarian trends in popular struggles.

The first time that contemporary Islamic fundamentalism emerged historically in the form of a militant political movement of a modern type was when the Muslim Brotherhood movement in Egypt attained impressive proportions in the aftermath of the Second World War. It grew to more than half a million members, and achieved such an overwhelming presence in Egyptian society that power seemed within its grasp. The conditions in which the movement expanded so explosively over a period of about twenty years were identical to those described above: a corrupt, despised Egyptian monarchy; widespread, deep poverty; British domination, made all the more unbearable by the presumed complicity of the British rulers of Mandate Palestine with the Zionist enterprise; the pusillanimity of the liberal, nationalist bourgeoisie represented by the Wafd Party; the weakness of the labour movement and marginality of the communist opposition, which had been harshly repressed in the 1920s.[26]

Yet in a short period in the 1950s and 1960s the Muslim Brotherhood movement was in its turn thrown back into marginality and contempt. Repression by Nasser's government was not the reason for this massive setback, although the repression was particularly harsh after Nasser's attempted assassination. Algeria under its military 'eradicators' provides proof, like General Mubarak's Egypt, that repression alone cannot succeed completely in wiping out a movement that is deeply rooted in part of the population and very determined to struggle by all means necessary, including the most violent ones. The deeper reason why Islamic fundamentalism withered away in Nasser's Egypt is the same reason that explains Nasser's considerable popularity, not only in his own country but also throughout the Arab world and the Islamic world beyond. Nasser was renowned throughout the vast Afro-Asiatic region that took the world political stage at the 1955 Bandung Conference.

The nationalization of the Suez Canal in 1956, followed by the tripartite Israeli-Franco-British aggression against Egypt, elevated Nasser to the status of hero of Third World liberation movements. He cultivated this role by becoming a champion and active promoter of Arab nationalism and Afro-Asiatic national struggles. He was able to win the support of the overwhelming majority of the Egyptian people by deciding to redistribute landed property and nationalize industry and foreign trade. Without a doubt he ushered in a period of great social progress in Egypt, notably with his democratic reform of the educational system. In short, by basing his rule solidly on a foundation of national, democratic and social aspirations, Nasser pulled the rug out from under his fundamentalist adversaries, and, incidentally, his communist adversaries as well.[27]

In order for Islamic fundamentalism as the mass phenomenon it has been since the 1970s to wither away lastingly as well – in the absence of an 'economic miracle' – new political movements would have to emerge that pose progressive political alternatives to the degenerate peripheral capitalism of the age of globalization/Americanization. They would have to prove themselves able to reconquer the terrain of national, democratic and social struggles. Such movements are not yet on the horizon. This is where the new Orientalist Gilles Kepel, despite his extensive knowledge of the subject, is mistaken in predicting the end of 'Islamism' in the near future.[28] His recent book *Jihad: Rise and Fall of Islamism* was reckless in announcing in its introduction:

> Islamist movements have entered ... a phase of decline that
> has been speeding up since the mid-1990s ... Today, in the
> year 2000, the exhaustion of Islamist political ideology and

mobilization is ushering in a third stage [following the stages of nationalism and 'Islamism'], a stage of transcendence. This phase, beginning as the twenty-first century begins, will doubtless be the phase in which the Islamic world lands with both feet in modernity, through unprecedented forms of fusion with the Western universe – notably through emigration and its effects and the revolution in information technology and telecommunications.[29]

It would be all too easy to wax ironic about the 'unprecedented form of fusion with the Western universe' that levelled the World Trade Center towers on 11 September 2001. The Muslim immigrant hijackers who diverted those airliners certainly showed that modern communication technology is an open book to them – thanks to an original combination of theology and technology, as the *Washington Post* so aptly put it.[30] But however flagrant Kepel's mistaken forecast, it is nonetheless instructive: it enables us to illustrate the thesis laid out above through a *reductio ad absurdum*. What in fact was his optimistic prediction based on?

Kepel was too quick to see the downward slide of certain forms of 'Islamism' that had arisen in the last quarter century as evidence of a general tendency toward decline. He took his desires for reality in a way that one can only call wishful thinking. We can in any event grant him, along with his inspirer Olivier Roy, the merit of rejecting the culturalist postulate that Islam and democracy are inherently incompatible.[31] But he has gone beyond asserting the compatibility of Islam and democracy – conditional, of course, on some necessary adaptations – to a naïve belief reminiscent of Francis Fukuyama's in the maturation of the historical conditions for the final victory of democracy and modernity in the Islamic world.[32] Kepel's approach is typically 'idealist' in the sense that the word is understood in the philosophy of history, or for that matter international relations theory. He turns up his nose at the structural prerequisites, socio-economic as well as political, for an extension of modernity in Muslim countries.

Instead he puts his faith, out of a certain kind of voluntarism, in the regenerative potential of regimes that are among the most corrupt and authoritarian on earth, in countries with crying, explosive social inequality:

> In the near future the ball will be in the court of the regimes that have emerged victorious from the confrontation with the ['Islamist'] current as a whole, which has been broken by the shock of armed violence or caught in the toils of co-optation in the corridors of power. At this turn of the century and millennium, it is up to them to integrate into society the social groups that had been marginalized since their countries won their independence. They must facilitate the birth of a sort of Muslim democracy, which would be able to combine culture, religion and political and economic modernity in an unprecedented way.
>
> This scenario presupposes that the rejuvenated elites that are taking power, from Mohammed VI's Morocco to Abdullah II's Jordan and from the military-technocratic entourage of Algerian President Bouteflika to that of Indonesian President 'Gus Dur' Wahid, will be capable of facing the future and 'sharing the pie' today so that it will be a bigger pie tomorrow.[33]

So much candour on Kepel's part is disconcerting. One would not expect an 'expert' like him to have illusions in the figures he mentions, who are no more capable of facilitating the birth of modernity or 'sharing the pie' than Ayatollah Khomeini was in his day of promoting human rights. (Michel Foucault may have succumbed to this illusion about Khomeini at one point. But then Foucault had two excuses: his ignorance about Iran and the Muslim world, and Khomeini's extraordinary popularity after leading a revolution that was impressive in many ways.[34])

## On Despotism in Muslim Countries

Like Fukuyama, the herald of the 'end of history' himself, Kepel has stuck to his thesis about the decline of 'Islamism'. Both of them contend that 11 September is nothing more than a sort of swan-song of this historical phenomenon, and thus does not weaken the case for the irresistible rise of modern liberal democracy. In Fukuyama's words:

> The clash consists of a series of rearguard actions from societies whose traditional existence is indeed threatened by modernization. The strength of the backlash reflects the severity of this threat. But time and resources are on the side of modernity, and I see no lack of a will to prevail in the United States today.[35]

And in Kepel's: 'This phenomenon of terrorist violence is the expression of a decline in the Islamist current's capacity to seize power ... What made the bin Laden phenomenon possible was the fragmentation of Islamism.'[36]

Kepel can even make the most of the fact that he had warned of new explosions in the near future if local 'elites', masters of their fate, did not undertake reforms. 'The leaders of this [Islamic] universe need more than ever to face up to their responsibilities, in a political conjuncture that is not unfavorable for them. They must act quickly.'[37] But this only shows the idealist character of his methodology.

His emphasis on the role of the free will of leaders of the kind mentioned above actually evades the issues, on the subjective level, of the social nature of the regimes, the social layers they depend on for their survival, and thus the interests they represent that inspire their endeavours. On the objective level, too, it evades the issues of the scope of their countries' social and political contradictions and their limited capacity to survive a confrontation with the opposition if ever they give free rein to it, as Algerian President Chadli Bendjedid and the Shah of Iran's experiments with conciliatory policies showed very clearly. Last but far from least, it evades the issue of how sharply Western hegemony itself puts the brakes on any democratization process in this part of the world. The new Orientalists tend in general to maintain silence on this issue.[38] As for Fukuyama, he rules it peremptorily out of court: 'These failures [of Muslim governments], and not anything that the outside world has done or refrained from doing, [are] the root cause of the Muslim world's stagnation.'[39]

I emphasized the importance of the West's role in an article published in *Le Monde Diplomatique* in June 1997, in which I explained:

> Of all the major geopolitical regions, the Arab world is the only one in which a relative reduction of the state's influence on the economy, though inaugurated by Anwar al-Sadat in Egypt as long ago as the early 1970s, has not seen an accompanying reduction of its control over politics. It is also the only one where civil society has been unable to wrest political expression from bureaucratic or despotic state control. The political regimes in the Arab world range from monarchies that are absolute *de jure* to republics that are absolutist *de facto*. In those Arab countries that lay claim to democracy, free elections are a fiction and, even in the best of cases, the freedoms granted are parsimonious, selective and closely supervised ...
>
> How are we to explain this Arab exception? And, more important, why is it so blatantly tolerated by those same big powers that preach democracy to the rest of the planet? ...
>
> Two basic factors explain the Arab despotic exception. The first is the curse of oil; the second is the nature of political opposition in the region, led by Islamic movements.
>
> Western sponsors' perpetuation, and in some cases establishment, of archaic tribal dynasties in the oil states of the Arabian peninsula contrasted strongly with colonialism's project of overturning traditional structures in other parts of

the world and setting up models emulating political modernity. The West's 'civilizing mission' in establishing state institutions did not apply to the oil states. Here on the contrary its project was to consolidate backwardness in order to guarantee the tutelary powers' unfettered exploitation of hydrocarbon resources. This was particularly the case in the Saudi kingdom.

Because the Saudi kingdom has the largest oil reserves in the world, it is one of the countries to which Washington attaches the greatest importance. The US has long directly controlled the kingdom's economic and security affairs, and maintained a structure of maximum social rigidity in order to foreclose any possibility of popular disorder. Special attention has been given to ensuring that no indigenous working class develops. The formula – identical to that applied in other oil states, but particularly absurd in Saudi Arabia given the size of the population – has been to favor the development of a privileged middle class among Saudi nationals, while relying essentially in the area of industrial production and manual labor on an immigrant workforce that is rigidly controlled and relatively restricted in numbers, thanks to the country's irrational recourse to the most advanced production technologies.

The structure of the Saudi army follows the same logic. Relatively small in number, in order to minimize the domestic risk of a republican coup d'état of the kind that brought down monarchies in Egypt, Iraq and Libya, it is impressively armed with equipment bought at prohibitive prices in what has proved to be a bonanza for Western cannon merchants. Thus, for a population four times the size of that of neighboring Jordan, the Saudi kingdom has barely twice as many personnel in its armed forces, but it spends 33 times what the Hashemite kingdom spends on its own military budget.

The Saudi army and National Guard, which are modeled on the country's tribal structures, are essentially a praetorian guard for the monarchy. Their effectiveness against external threats is very doubtful, and in any event is quite out of proportion to their costs, which are two and a half times greater than those of Israel's army ...

This kingdom, so closely allied to the US that US officials feel free to debate its budgetary policy, is the antithesis of democracy. It is a kingdom where the Koran and the sharia are the only basic law, run by ultra-orthodox Wahhabis. It is undoubtedly the most fundamentalist state in the world, the most totalitarian in political and cultural terms, and the most oppressive of the female half of the population. It makes Iranian society look relatively liberal, pluralist and freedom loving toward its women by comparison.

Here we see the hypocrisy of those who are perfectly ready to condemn fundamentalism in the name of secularism and democracy whenever it takes on an anti-Western tinge, but who are equally happy to enjoy and exploit their lucrative friendship with the Saudis. One can easily see why the peoples of the Arab world saw the proclamations of the anti-Iraq coalition during the Gulf War as mendacious and inadmissible, given that this same coalition, with the United States at its head, was trumpeting its defense of democratic values from bases in the Saudi kingdom and with Saudi help.

So one of the basic reasons for the despotic exception in the Arab world is that the West could not promote democratic values in the Arab world – even if only in words – without running the risk of damaging its protégés in the Gulf.

But there is also a second fundamental reason: the burgeoning growth of the other, Iranian-style, radically anti-Western face of fundamentalism. Here the West is reaping what it helped to sow ...

After so many years of anti-communist and anti-nationalist struggle conducted under the banner of Islam rather than liberal democracy, bankrupt nationalism and an impotent left have left the door wide open to Islamic fundamentalism.

Riyadh and Washington had thoroughly greased the slippery slope of religion, which lent itself most readily therefore to nationalist and social popular challenges.

There followed a long period of hesitancy, during which the Saudi rulers and their US advisers imagined that the contagion could be contained by playing up the specifically Shiite nature of Iran, and by playing 'Sunni moderates' off against 'Shiite extremists'. Riyadh continued to play godfather to Sunni fundamentalist movements, in particular the currents emerging from the Muslim Brotherhood. However, this new tactic proved to be equally disastrous. In 1990, at the moment when the Gulf crisis put Iraq and Saudi Arabia in opposing camps, major sections of the Sunni fundamentalist movement, which Riyadh had supported, took Iraq's side in order not to cut themselves off from their social base. This was a stinging fiasco for the Saudi monarchy.

With the collapse of the USSR in 1991 leaving only a remnant of communism behind, Washington decreed that the West's public enemy number one was now to be Iranian-style radical Islam. We had thus moved in a brief period from the 'end of history' to the 'clash of civilizations'. Needless to say, the same hypocrisy that made the Saudi monarchy an ally of Western civilization has continued unabated. Its most recent 'success' has been in Afghanistan, where Washington and Riyadh's collusion with the Taliban has been widely reported.

Thus the fact that anti-Western Islamic fundamentalism has become the main channel for popular resistance in the Arab world combined with the Saudi monarchy's own anti-democratic influence to ensure that from 1990 onwards – unlike the processes of political evolution elsewhere in the world – the Arab variant of the 'new world order' was still to be built on despotism.[40]

Although it keeps quiet about it, the United States is recycling the same arguments today in the face of anti-Western Islamic fundamentalism that they used in the past to justify their support for Pinochet-style dictatorships, described euphemistically as 'authoritarian'. The pretext was that authoritarian regimes were preferable to the alternative possibility in this scheme: a slide, even by democratic electoral means, toward Marxist regimes, described as at least potentially 'totalitarian'. Totalitarian regimes, according to the rationale, would be difficult if not impossible to overthrow.[41]

This was one of the consequences of what Samuel Huntington, using his own interpretive matrix, calls 'the democracy paradox: adoption by non-Western societies of Western democratic institutions encourages and gives access to power to nativist and anti-Western political movements.'[42] For the same reasons, Bush Junior's 'war on terrorism' today includes support for 'democrats' with remarkable credentials, such as a general who overthrew Pakistan's elected government by means of a putsch, or an Uzbek autocrat carrying on the repressive practices of the former Soviet regime in a mafia-style capitalist version.

### Neither Fascist nor Progressive

One of the main functions of the analogy that George W. Bush, following many others, makes between radical, anti-Western Islamic fundamentalism and 'totalitarianism' is to justify continued support for 'authoritarian' regimes in the Muslim world. As Bush put it in his speech to Congress on 20 September 2001: 'These terrorists ... are the heirs of all the murderous ideologies of the 20th century. By sacrificing human life to serve their radical visions – by abandoning every value except the will to power – they follow in the path of fascism, and Nazism, and totalitarianism.'[43]

Francis Fukuyama, who made the analogy between Islamic fundamentalism and totalitarianism in his unjustly famous book[44] and is still propagating it, has a paradox of his own, though a lesser one. Through continually restating and overstating this same theme, Fukuyama has ended up objectively justifying his own government's blockage of the world's triumphal march toward liberal democracy, whose proclamation has gained him so much access to overblown celebrity in the last few years. For a man who saw the fall of 'communism' as 'the end of history', he has managed to refute his own argument with remarkable efficiency. Now he portrays radical Islamic fundamentalism, which he calls 'Islamo-fascism', as in some respects a bigger challenge to liberal democracy than the challenge faced during the Cold War: 'The Islamo-fascist sea within which the terrorists swim constitutes an ideological challenge that is in some ways more basic than the one posed by communism.'[45] Fukuyama has suddenly discovered, in a kind of intellectual hara-kiri, that 'unfortunately there is no inevitability to historical progress.'[46]

To be sure, leaving aside the differences between the societies and cultures concerned, one can identify common characteristics of these two historical phenomena, fascism and anti-Western Islamic fundamentalism. Each has a petit bourgeois and plebeian social base, a deeply reactionary social programme, a fanatical character and a propensity to violence. But the differences outweigh the similarities. Unlike historical fascism, anti-Western Islamic fundamentalism is not an acute manifestation of an imperial policy and a reaction to the rise of the workers movement. Rather, it is an acute manifestation of opposition to imperialist domination and to the corrupt bourgeois regimes on which that domination depends.[47] When a political identification between fascism and radical Islamic fundamentalism emerges from a left-wing discourse, it is generally meant to legitimize either support to local dictatorships (as in the case of the Algerian *communistes éradicateurs*, leftists who backed the military's dirty war against the Islamic opposition) or support to Western powers' policies (as with those who backed George W. Bush's 'crusade' against Afghanistan in the name of democracy and women's liberation).

The political inanity of identifying 'Islamism' with fascism is most obvious of all in the case of the radical Islamic opposition to the Saudi monarchy, the very opposition that has acquired Osama bin Laden as its poster boy. Anyone who maintains that the chief motive of the virulent opposition to the Saudi ruling family is the desire to create a 'totalitarian' regime is in effect decking out the Saudi kingdom in democratic finery. The fact is that up until 1990 bin Laden was acting on behalf of the Saudi-Wahhabite regime, even if his ties with the regime went by way of his family and even if, as he has claimed, he had long been a critic of Riyadh's links to the United States.[48] US troops' intervention in his country, not any imaginary democratization of the regime, inspired his turn against the Saudi rulers.

On the other hand, a close look at this same moment when bin Laden turned against the Saudi rulers shows that it is just as foolish to see any progressive virtue – even an 'objectively anti-imperialist' significance – in his fanatical fundamentalist jihad. Bin Laden as head of al-Qa'ida was in fact ready to take on the defence of the Saudi kingdom, a US vassal, against Saddam Hussein's nationalist Iraq. One of his followers has told the story:

> Late 1989, after the Soviet withdrawal from Afghanistan, he went to the kingdom in an ordinary trip. There he was banned from travel and was trapped in the kingdom. The Soviet withdrawal might have been a factor but the main reason for the travel ban [was] his intentions to start a new 'front' of jihad in South Yemen. In addition, he embarrassed the regime by lectures and speeches warning of impending invasion by Saddam. At that time the regime was [on] very good terms with Saddam. He was instructed officially to keep [a] low profile and not to give public talks. Despite the travel ban he was not hostile to the regime at this stage. Indeed, he presented a written advice in the form of a detailed, personal, private and confidential letter to the king [a] few weeks before the Iraqi invasion of Kuwait.
>
> He reacted swiftly to [the] Iraqi invasion and saw it [as] fulfilling his prophecy. He immediately forwarded another

letter to the king suggesting in detail how to protect the country from potentially advancing Iraqi forces. In addition to [the] many military tactics suggested, he volunteered to bring all the Arab mujahedin to defend the kingdom. That letter was presented in the first few days of the incident, and the regime response was [to give it] consideration!

While he was expecting some call to mobilize his men and equipment he heard the news that transferred [sic] his life completely. The Americans are coming. He always describes that moment as [a] shocking moment.[49]

His megalomaniacal, xenophobic *amour propre* severely wounded, bin Laden became from that moment on a sworn enemy of the Saudi monarchy and its Western sponsors. His arguments against the presence of US troops in the kingdom have been thoroughly reactionary, fanatically religious and sexist. His statement in 1998, when the TV channel al-Jazeera gave him an opportunity to reach a broad Arabic-speaking audience, provides a good illustration:

> They want to strip us of our manhood, and we believe that we are men, and Muslim men, who have to protect the most important sanctuary in the universe, the sacred Kaaba, which we have the honor of protecting, instead of having American, Jewish and Christian, women soldiers come ... The rulers of this region may have lost their manhood, and believe that people are women, and by God even the decent women among Muslims' women refuse to be defended by these American and Jewish whores.[50]

Osama bin Laden is far from being the expression of a progressive revolt against the Saudi monarchy and its sponsors. Rather, he is the standard bearer of the most reactionary Wahhabite ideology, that is, the extreme version of the kingdom's own dominant ideology. Admittedly his location in the spotlight of media attention as the US public enemy number one has earned him the allegiance or sympathy of a considerable number of the 'wretched of the earth' – including the sympathy of people who legitimately hate US hegemony and its local relays throughout the Islamic world (just think of how the Palestinians feel, for example) and far beyond it.

Inside the Saudi kingdom itself the same thing is happening that has occurred in many other Arab and Muslim countries, but pushed to the furthest extreme. The whips of the religious police, the *mutawwi'ah* of the Committee for the Prevention of Vice and Promotion of Virtue, have beaten into the population a totalitarian ban on any form of ideological, political or cultural expression outside the bounds of the dominant Wahhabism. Repression has made Wahhabism itself the most 'natural' form for popular resentment to express itself. This resentment is directed at the harsh oppression that reigns in the kingdom, the profound corruption of the royal family, and the protection it enjoys from the United States.

Incidentally, this is not the first time that the Saudi monarchy has experienced a blowback from the Islamic fundamentalism that it has done so much to disseminate throughout the Islamic world. Two successive waves of anti-Western fundamentalist resurgence have struck the kingdom in turn. In 1979 the impact of the Iranian revolution was felt not only through a revolt by the Shiite minority in the kingdom's eastern province but also, much more spectacularly, through an uprising in Mecca by a group of Wahhabite extremists. Led by a man named Juhayman of the Al Utayba tribe, one of the kingdom's largest, the rebels were disgusted at the royal family's corruption.[51] In the wake of the Gulf war and deployment and later stationing of US troops in the kingdom, the monarchy came up against another Wahhabite challenge. In 1992 a group of ulemas criticized the regime's corruption and the continued presence of US troops on the 'sacred' soil of the Saudi kingdom, the guardian of Islam's holy cities. Then, in 1994, an insurrection broke out in the city of Burayda, following the arrest of two dissident ulemas, and ended with several hundred arrests.

## Bin Laden's Duel with Washington

Osama bin Laden's turn against the government of his country, which he had to flee for good in 1991 after his return from Afghanistan, and against its US overlord is part of the second wave of ultra-puritan religious opposition to the Saudi monarchy. Bin Laden brought to it the know-how and trained personnel acquired in the long experience of the Afghanistan war. He would use this against US troops, which he saw as a heathen occupation force rather than as an imperialist one. In November 1995 a first attack killed five US soldiers and two Indian workers in Riyadh. (The four presumed authors of the attack were decapitated.) Then in June 1996 came the suicide attack on the Khobar Towers in Dhahran, which caused nineteen deaths among US troops. That same year Saudi and US pressure on Sudan, where bin Laden had taken refuge, forced him to go back to Afghanistan. There he reorganized the al-Qa'ida network and sealed an alliance with the Taliban.

At this moment a fully fledged war was already being waged, sometimes covertly, sometimes spectacularly, between the Islamic fundamentalists and the US government. Attacks on US troops attributed to the bin Laden network took place in Yemen in 1992 and again in Somalia in 1993. The first attempt at destroying the World Trade Center towers, in 1993, would be attributed to bin Laden as well, after the operation's organizer, Ramzi Yousef, was arrested. Other actions would follow, including attacks on Saudi soil. On the opposite side, US and Saudi secret services, working together with their Pakistani counterparts, attempted several times to assassinate bin Laden. The CIA set up a thousand-strong mercenary force, equipped with helicopters and off-road vehicles, that attacked one of the al-Qa'ida network's Afghan bases in July 1997 in an effort to kidnap or kill him.[52]

The rout of US troops in Somalia in 1994–5, added to the earlier victory over Soviet troops in Afghanistan, gave bin Laden a new surge of confidence. He decided to fight his former allies, themselves determined to eliminate him, to the bitter end. In February 1998 he proclaimed a 'World Islamic Front for Jihad Against the Jews and Crusaders'. Its first statement declared that it was legitimate and imperative to 'kill Americans and their allies, military and civilian', in the name of the Muslim religion. Several themes appear in this initial declaration that have been reiterated many times since, including three denunciations: of the presence of US troops on the holy soil of the Arabian peninsula; of the murderous embargo against the Iraqi Muslim population; and of the massacre of the Palestinian Muslim population by the 'Crusader-Zionist alliance'.

The most spectacular episodes of the next moves in this war between the Islamic fundamentalist David and the US imperialist Goliath are well known: the attacks on the US embassies in Kenya and Tanzania in August 1998; the subsequent launch of US cruise missiles at Afghanistan and Sudan; the suicide attack on the destroyer USS *Cole* in Yemen in October 2000; the suicide attacks on 11 September 2001; and the US aggression against Afghanistan launched on 7 October 2001. The list is certainly not complete yet.

One could ask in this connection why the Clinton Administration, which was waging this fierce war for many years, did not support the Northern Alliance in Afghanistan rather than shooting off useless missiles at the poor country. Contrary to what admirers of Commander Massoud may have thought, it was not out of lack of daring. Its motives show considerably more political foresight than the current crop of swashbuckling sponsors of proxy wars seem to have.[53]

> Interceding on the side of the Northern Alliance would have meant backing the losing side and casting lots with corrupt and brutal militias, a former official said: not 'white knight versus black knight' but 'dark grey knight against black knight.' Albright said the idea was unworthy of serious thought. 'We all were operating with the history of Afghanistan and the unintended consequences of getting involved' in the 1980s, Albright recalled. 'We armed all those people and provided

them with the Stingers. For us to get involved in a civil war on behalf of the Northern Alliance would have been insane.'[54]

Other episodes in the war between the United States and the al-Qa'ida network are less well known. For example, few people know that the Pakistani secret service and the CIA set up a new commando force in 1999 with the mission of capturing or killing bin Laden in Afghanistan. (The project was suspended because of Pervez Musharraf's coup.)[55] Nor do many people know about the so-called rendition operations, in which the United States prevails on a submissive or venal government to illegally turn over to Washington individuals whom it considers prejudicial to its interests.[56] In other cases 'rendition' means turning over individuals who cannot be punished under US laws to countries that are much less squeamish about human rights. To cite one example among dozens: the CIA and Albanian secret service kidnapped five Egyptian Islamic fundamentalists in Albania in 1998 and flew them to Egypt, where they were brought before a military tribunal and executed.[57]

All sorts of lunatic ideas have been spouted since 11 September about this merciless, violent confrontation between the two former allies. One of the theories that has done the rounds the most (based on an openly racist, right-wing 'anti-Islamism' or on a left-wing 'anti-Islamism' paved with good intentions) is that the Saudi kingdom itself is pulling the strings behind bin Laden. This absurd idea is the fruit of a phantasmagoric vision of the world.[58] It obscures the fact that the Saudi regime is the one most threatened by bin Laden's activities, and that this is one of the greatest worries of its godfathers in Washington. The Saudi monarchy itself, eager to foster the illusion that it can hold its own against its US protector, is all too pleased with this kind of rumour.[59]

Similarly, bin Laden's wealth (some media outlets even insist that he is a 'billionaire')[60] is emphasized constantly, to the point that some people even think they can analyse the al-Qa'ida network's motives in terms of 'capitalist interests'.[61] This view completely misses the fact that one of the main reasons for bin Laden's popularity is his (not undeserved) reputation as the son of a rich family who has sacrificed his fortune, lives in poverty, and has risked his life many times for the cause he fanatically believes in.

One individual's sociological profile can never sum up the sociology of a movement that he inspires or leads. In any event, the bulk of al-Qa'ida's members certainly do not consist of billionaires or millionaires. They fit quite neatly into the typical social profile of militant Islamic fundamentalist movements. The fact that fifteen out of the nineteen September 11 hijackers were 'Saudis' does not imply at all that they were oil sheiks. According to the investigations carried out by US services: 'Most hailed from poor villages where fundamentalism thrives. But their families appeared to be on the upper rungs; their fathers were religious leaders, school principals, shopkeepers, and businessmen.'[62]

It cannot be news to anybody – certainly not to the present author, as the 1981 theses cited above show – that the social base of Islamic fundamentalism is not made up exclusively of poor or indigent people. Many of them belong to the middle classes. It is nonetheless important to understand the anomie,[63] the disorientating loss of reference points, that has struck these members of the middle classes, of rural or urban traditional, petit bourgeois origin. These social layers have faced first the oil boom and then the oil crisis, deepening social inequality, and many young people's fear of a work life threatened by 'postgraduate unemployment'. This anomie has long been fuelling resentment, which is easily turned against the powers that be. It has an affinity for the ideologies that lend themselves most easily to expressing protest.

The key factor is not individuals' living standards in absolute terms but the prospects they have for rising relative living standards in the future; that is, the gap between their real prospects and their aspirations. Emile Durkheim explained this very well when he traced 'anomic suicide' back to its socio-economic causes.[64] Without grasping the meaning of this anomie, one risks coming up with a static, social determinist explanation of a phenomenon like Islamic fundamentalism. Radicalized Islamic fundamentalism is no more the spontaneous emanation of poverty, actually, than it 'results from wealth', as Daniel Pipes, a member of the US Middle East policy establishment, seems to believe. Pipes makes a travesty of a series of facts and figures in an attempt to shore up his thesis, which at bottom comes down to the most caricatured version of the 'clash of civilizations'.[65]

The Egyptian Mohammed Atta, the main organizer of the 11 September attacks – of whom Terry McDermott published a remarkable profile in the *Los Angeles Times* – also belonged to a comfortable middle-class family of rural origin. He was a brilliant student; after beginning architecture school in Cairo he was able to go on to study urban planning in Hamburg, Germany. In 1995 he won a German grant to study the Egyptian government's plans to convert the part of Cairo called the 'Islamic city' into a tourist complex. He went there accompanied by two other students, both German, one of whom was named Ralph Bodenstein. The episode that McDermott recounts is revealing about the – incidentally, widespread – grounds that can nurture anti-American resentment in a young postgraduate Egyptian and pious Muslim who is witnessing the grievous spectacle of his own country:

> What the three young architects found appalled them. The government planned to 'restore' the area by removing many of the people who lived there, evicting the onion and garlic sellers, repairing the old buildings and bringing in troupes of actors to play the real people they would displace.
>
> Bodenstein described what happened: 'We had a very critical discussion with the municipality. They didn't understand our concerns. They wanted to do their work, dress people in costumes. They thought it was a good idea and couldn't imagine why we would object.'
>
> It was Atta's first professional contact with the Egyptian bureaucracy and it distressed him, Bodenstein said.
>
> 'Mohammed was very, very critical of the planning

administration, the nepotism. He had begun to make inquiries about getting a job after school, and he had difficulty finding anything. He did not belong to the network, where jobs were handed down from one generation to the next, to political allies. Mohammed was very idealistic, humanistic; he had social ideals to fulfill.'

Atta's complaints about the difficulty of finding a decent job were not unique. Egypt's ambitious, virtually free system of higher education pumps out many more graduates than the economy can handle. The more education you have, the less likely you are to find a job. According to one 1998 study, those with graduate degrees are 32 times more likely to be unemployed than illiterate people are.

Bodenstein said Atta's critique of the government grew more expansive as the study project went on. He said the government's redevelopment plans would turn the old city into an Islamic Disneyland. Such Western influences, he said, were the result of the government's eagerness to be allied with the United States.[66]

Unlike Osama bin Laden, who is an atypical figure in many respects, Mohammed Atta is entirely representative – almost a perfect statistical portrait – of the young graduates who make up the intellectual elite, the 'organic intellectuals', of this petit bourgeois and plebeian Muslim current. Their rebellion against corrupt, intolerable, US-sponsored regimes has been taking them for three decades now down the path of Islamic fundamentalism.

# THREE

# Hatred, Barbarisms, Asymmetry and Anomie

There is no need to resort to fantastic theories or philosophical divagations in order to understand Osama bin Laden's motives. He is a religious fundamentalist, not a nihilist. He certainly would not identify with Nietzschean or Heideggerian versions of nihilism, except perhaps for their contempt for the 'last men', which is not unique to nihilists. Nor will anyone understand the source of bin Laden's acts by reading Dostoevsky, as onetime 'new philosopher' André Glucksmann has tried to do.

Glucksmann's use of the word nihilist, like Bush's use of terrorist, has a clear ideological function. In his words, it 'gives a juridical basis to a universal alliance against terrorism – understood, we should be clear, in its nihilist variant.'[1] Like the pirates of yore, Glucksmann explains, bin Laden must be declared an 'enemy of humanity' (*hostis generis humani*), an outlaw who is a legitimate target for capture 'dead or alive'. Glucksmann proceeds to add immediately, 'The American president's repeated expression is traditional and welcome, despite the incomprehension and contemptuous smiles of listeners with short memories.'[2] What happy memory can the expression 'dead or alive' possibly evoke in André Glucksmann's mind? Admittedly he can avail himself of the *fatwa* issued by Michael Walzer, the great ayatollah of 'just war' theory: Walzer has justified assassinating the political leaders of terrorist organizations on the grounds that they are 'hard to mark off [from military leaders], and we are not planning on negotiations [with them].'[3]

In reality, leaving aside superficial similarities among different forms of conspiracy, bin Laden's world-view does not have much in common with that of the resolutely atheist terrorists of nineteenth-century tsarist Russia – nor even with the caricature that Dostoevsky gave of their world-view in his novel *The Possessed*. Unlike Dostoevsky's characters, bin Laden certainly did not aim at spreading 'complete disbelief in everything' so as 'to reduce the country at a given moment, if need be, to desperation'.[4] Bin Laden's aim was to terrorize the US government and people to the point that they would have to grant some clearly defined demands. He also sought to galvanize Muslim peoples while propagating his own fanatical, fundamentalist faith. One need only listen to or read bin Laden's own explanations. A very complete exposition can be found in his statements filmed by an ABC network reporter in southern Afghanistan in May 1998. The first part of the videotape, the transcript of which the PBS network has made public, consists of an illuminating discussion between Washington's public enemy number one and several of his disciples.

## Hatred and Strategy

Osama bin Laden's hatred of the United States is equalled only by his hatred for the Saudi monarchy. Seeking to overthrow the Saudis, he knew quite well that this was impossible while they enjoy US protection. His primary goal was thus to force US troops to withdraw from the Saudi kingdom and put an end to the protection they provide to its execrable regime:

> The call to wage war against America was made because America has spearheaded the crusade against the Islamic nation, sending tens of thousands of its troops to the land of the two Holy Mosques over and above its meddling in its affairs and its politics, and its support of the oppressive, corrupt and tyrannical regime that is in control. These are the reasons behind the singling out of America as a target.[5]

This was bin Laden's only openly proclaimed objective. His acts were meant to attain it by means of terrorist pressure, or failing that, to win ideological hegemony over 'Saudi', Arab and Muslim public opinion by means of this spectacular battle. All the other causes he invoked, like the fate of the Iraqis or Palestinians, he was using only as polemical arguments – and of course in order to motivate his non-'Saudi' followers. Whenever anyone has questioned his failure to distinguish between military and civilian targets, bin Laden has consistently answered that the United States and its Israeli ally are not hindered by scruples about killing civilians, and children in particular, in Iraq and Palestine.

Nevertheless, in the months leading up to 11 September, bin Laden began to pay much more attention to the Palestinians' situation, in connection with what has been called the 'second Intifada'. Then, in a video message sent out on 7 October, the day that Operation Enduring Freedom began in Afghanistan, he promoted Palestine to an immediate objective of his struggle – just as Saddam Hussein did in 1990 in order to win as much support as possible by using the Islamic world's single most popular cause:

> As for America, I address to it and to its people these carefully weighed words: I swear by God Almighty, who raised the heavens without pillars, that neither America nor those who inhabit America will be able to dream of security before we are really living in security in Palestine, and before all the miscreant armies have left the land of Mohammed, may God's blessing and protection be upon him.[6]

With more foresight than Saddam Hussein, however, bin Laden had no illusions about the possibility of defeating the United States in a head-on confrontation. He understood that, given overwhelming US military superiority, the only way to strike violent, painful blows against it was to resort to what Washington has since 1997 officially called 'asymmetric means', defined as 'unconventional approaches that avoid or undermine our strengths while exploiting our vulnerabilities.'[7] Unable to wage 'the mother of all battles' against the United States, bin Laden's followers have undeniably succeeded in inflicting 'the mother of all terrorist attacks' on it.

This method of action serves entirely rational ends, contrary to what many would like to believe. Bin Laden hoped to create a situation in which the US population, weary of bearing the brunt of its government's involvement in a part of the world that it has no more interest in than it did in Vietnam thirty years ago, would put pressure on its government to disengage and get out. This is why he directed his warnings, as in his 7 October message, not only to the US government and its Western allies but also to their peoples. He did so even more clearly in his 1998 statements, which called people to attention:

> The Western regimes and the government of the United States of America bear the blame for what might happen. If their people do not wish to be harmed inside their very own countries, they should seek to elect governments that are truly representative of them and that can protect their interests.[8]

In his direct responses to the ABC network reporter, after accusing the Clinton Administration of representing 'the Jews' interests', bin Laden warned the people of the United States:

> If the present injustice continues with the wave of national consciousness, it will inevitably move the battle to American soil, just as Ramzi Yousef [organizer of the 1993 attack on the World Trade Center] and others have done. This is my message to the American people. I urge them to find a serious administration that acts in their interest and does not attack people and violate their honor and pilfer their wealth.[9]

Yet a few months later, after the US strikes against Iraq in the course of Operation Desert Fox, bin Laden changed his tone. He said on the al-Jazeera network:

> Every American man is an enemy for us, whether he is fighting directly against us or just paying taxes. You may have heard

in the last few days that about three fourths of the American people support Clinton's strikes against Iraq. A people whose president's popularity goes up when he bombs innocent civilians ... is a degenerate people that has no sense of values.[10]

Bin Laden seems to have grasped a key aspect of any strategy for resisting the United States: the United States cannot be defeated militarily, and the most effective way to get its government to yield is through US public opinion. But on the other hand, he made two fatal mistakes. First, he underestimated the importance of the Arabian peninsula, the world's largest reservoir of oil, for the US ruling class. This mistake, which Saddam Hussein made before him, leads to an underestimation of US rulers' determination to shrink from nothing in defending their interests in this region, which is much more important in their eyes than Indochina could ever have been. It goes without saying that Arabia matters infinitely more to them than Somalia, which bin Laden cited illusively as evidence of US 'weakness'.[11]

Bin Laden's second fatal error was to have thought that by attacking US civilians in such a criminal, devastating way, he would succeed in convincing them to force their rulers to disengage. Hamas's Palestinian suicide bombers make the same mistake. In both cases, terrorist actions against civilians only make the targeted populations stand firmly behind their rulers' most reactionary, brutal policies. The Vietnamese succeeded in forcing the withdrawal of US troops from their country in 1973 only by combining incontestably legitimate forms of military struggle against the occupying army with a discourse addressed to the US people, appealing to its sense of justice rather than to its fears. The moral superiority of the Vietnamese struggle largely made up for the inferiority of their military means.

Having said this, we must add that Palestinian, 'Saudi' or other suicide bombers, who give up their lives in order to kill as many people as possible in the enemy country, are not all necessarily making political or strategic calculations of this kind. But neither are they motivated, except in a secondary way, by faith that they are earning a passport to paradise. Still less are they motivated by hatred for the 'values' that George Bush claims to represent. Like other candidates for martyrdom, believers or atheists, they are moved essentially by implacable hatred called forth by brutal, murderous, cynical, arrogant domination by the greatest power on the planet. This hatred explains the great popularity of the 11 September attacks in the Third World and beyond.[12]

> Hate as a factor in the struggle, intransigent hatred for the enemy that takes one beyond the natural limitations of a human being and converts one into an effective, violent, selective, cold, killing machine. Our soldiers must be like that; a people without hate cannot triumph over a brutal enemy.
>
> We must carry the war as far as the enemy carries it: into his home, into his places of recreation, make it total. He must be prevented from having a moment's peace, a moment's quiet outside the barracks and even inside them. Attack him wherever he may be; make him feel like a hunted animal wherever he goes. Then his morale will begin to decline. He will become even more bestial, but the signs of the coming decline will appear.[13]

Osama bin Laden? No – Ernesto Che Guevara, in the most famous of his writings, his message to the Tricontinental in 1967, a few months before his tragic death.

We have seen, however, that hatred is too often blind, and a very poor counsellor. The 11 September bombers, as they steered their hijacked planes toward their monumental targets, probably experienced the ecstasy that Malraux attributes in *Man's Estate* to Chen, the Chinese Communist who throws himself, 'eyes firmly shut', a bomb under his arm, onto Chiang Kai-shek's car.[14] Chen has more in common with the Muslim suicide bombers than Dostoevsky's characters do. The bombers cast down the twin pillars of the World Trade Center the way Samson does in the Bible, motivated by the same kind of hatred of the enemy and thirst for vengeance:

> ... [A]ll the lords of the Philistines were there; and there were upon the roof about three thousand men and women, that beheld while Samson made sport.

And Samson called unto the Lord, and said, O Lord God, remember me, I pray thee, and strengthen me, I pray thee, only this once, O God, that I may be at once avenged of the Philistines for my two eyes.

And Samson took hold of the two middle pillars upon which the house stood, and on which it was borne up, of the one with his right hand, and of the other with his left.

And Samson said, Let me die with the Philistines. And he bowed himself with all his might; and the house fell upon the lords, and upon all the people that were therein. So the dead which he slew at his death were more than they which he slew in his life.[15]

A terrible vengeance, but how pointless! In the last analysis, the 11 September bombers caused the death of many more of 'their own people'. Afghans, Palestinians, Chechens and other Muslims all fell victim to even more terrible acts of vengeance on the part of the Empire and its allies, which burst out in a rage and were freer to kill than they had ever been before. Guevara was wrong: the ferocious beast only loses its morale if it is run to earth by one stronger than it is, by an enemy that it is powerless against – and the strong will always run the weak to earth in the end. When it is bloodily wounded by a creature weaker than itself, the ferocious beast only becomes even more bestial. In this case the Clausewitzean dynamic of going to extremes is set off:

[I]n such dangerous things as War, the errors which proceed from a spirit of benevolence are the worst. As the use of physical power to the utmost extent by no means excludes the cooperation of the intelligence, it follows that he who uses force unsparingly, without reference to the bloodshed involved, must obtain a superiority if his adversary uses less vigour in its application ...

... [I]t is to no purpose, it is even against one's own interest, to turn away from the consideration of the real nature of the affair because the horror of its elements excites repugnance.[16]

*The Clash of Barbarisms*

What a huge misinterpretation it is to mistake something for a 'clash of civilizations' that is quite evidently a clash of barbarisms! Admittedly, Samuel Huntington was careful to make clear in his book that he makes a distinction between two meanings of the word 'civilization', one meaning that makes sense as a plural and the other only as a singular. The two can even contradict each other, he says, inasmuch as 'a civilization in the plural sense could in fact be quite uncivilized in the singular sense.'[17] But this oversimplified distinction, founded on, among other things, a reductionist reading of Fernand Braudel,[18] sidesteps the problem of the close connection between the two notions. Civilization in the singular (which we shall capitalize from now on), in the sense of a refinement of customs, mastery of aggressiveness and pacification of relationships among individuals and states, must be understood as a process. It is not yet completed but still 'underway',[19] to cite a famous analysis by Norbert Elias that Huntington fails to mention.

In adopting Elias's analysis, we must at the same time avoid the Western ethnocentrism that Elias hardly escapes from at all. In this way we can easily show that there is in fact a 'civilizing process' at work on the scale of the historical long range within various different civilizations, in their autonomous development as well as in their mutual interactions. But we must not lose sight of the corollary of this historical process, which can be demonstrated just as easily: each step in the advance of Civilization gives rise to specific modalities of Barbarism. Each civilization produces its own specific forms of barbarism. These are not aberrations in the 'civilizing process' – as Enzo Traverso rightly emphasizes in a brilliant short work inspired by Hannah Arendt on the European genealogy of Nazi violence – but 'an expression of one of its potentialities, one of its faces, one of its possible offshots ...'[20] This is why it is even more correct to borrow Herbert Marcuse's expression and speak of a 'dialectic of civilization':

> The destructiveness of the present stage reveals its full

significance only if the present is measured, not in terms of past stages, but in terms of its own potentialities. There is more than a quantitative difference in whether wars are waged by professional armies in confined spaces, or against entire populations on a global scale; whether technical inventions that could make the world free from misery are used for the conquest or for the creation of suffering; whether thousands are slain in combat or millions scientifically exterminated with the help of doctors and engineers; whether exiles can find refuge across the frontiers or are chased around the earth; whether people are naturally ignorant or are being *made* ignorant by their daily intake of information and entertainment.[21]

One should also distinguish therefore between Barbarism in the singular and barbarisms in the plural. Marx was well aware of this in his article on the Indian Mutiny:

> Cruelty, like every other thing, has its fashion, changing according to time and place. Caesar, the accomplished scholar, candidly narrates how he ordered many thousand Gallic warriors to have their right hands cut off. Napoleon would have been ashamed to do this. He preferred dispatching his own French regiments, suspected of republicanism, to St Domingo, there to die of the blacks [*sic*] and the plague.[22]

Each civilization has its own barbarism. Some people cut throats, a traditional Afghan murder method imported into Algeria by veterans of the anti-Soviet war, and symbolized by the 11 September bombers' box-cutter knives. Others 'cut daisies': they kill massively at a distance using 'daisy cutters', the most deadly 'conventional' (15,000-pound) bombs in existence. Some people hijack airliners so as to use them as missiles to murder civilians. Others launch cruise missiles in 'surgical strikes' that are to surgery what chain saws are to scalpels.

Some people seek to impress as many people as possible with the spectacle of their victims. Others imitate Molière's hypocritical

Tartuffe and order the media to cover up the carnage wreaked by their vengeance: 'I can't bear to see it. Such pernicious sights give rise to sinful thoughts.'[23] Hypocrisy, indeed, is not only the homage that vice pays to virtue, but also the homage that Barbarism pays to Civilization. Even the Nazis hid their cold-blooded enterprise of extermination behind the barbed wire of their camps.

How, then, must we judge the fact that Donald Rumsfeld's Pentagon boasted at first about the dehumanizing way it transported and housed prisoners in Camp X-Ray in Guantánamo Bay? These men were captured in what is officially known as the 'war on terrorism' in Afghanistan, yet in defiance of all logic they were denied the status of prisoners of war. Rumsfeld thought he could justify the way they were treated by describing them as 'unlawful combatants'. This juridical innovation sounds like a 'civilized' equivalent under the 'rule of law' of what *Untermenschen* (subhumans) were for the Nazi state. Primo Levi has movingly described how even these *Untermenschen* were classified at Auschwitz, with the wretched prisoners on the bottom rung being nicknamed *Muselmänner* (Muslims).[24]

Today in the United States thousands of other *Muselmänner*, Muslim immigrants, have found themselves caught in the meshes of post-11 September repression and collective paranoia. Hundreds of them are still being arbitrarily detained, often in secret, in violation of the right to be 'secure in their persons' included in the US Constitution and the 1948 Universal Declaration of Human Rights.

Thousands of civilians were killed directly in one morning in New York; tens of thousands of civilians have been killed indirectly each year in Iraq for over ten years. This is the scale of comparison of each barbarism's murders. The richer and more powerful a civilization is, the deadlier its barbarism. A few decades ago in powerful Germany, the Nazis invented industrialized genocide. Today the rich countries are guilty, through industrialized failure to assist, of 'biogenocide' at the expense of Black Africans and other miserable people with AIDS. Whether this is evidence of the progress of Civilization is open to doubt.

We can imagine what Michel Foucault, one of the best at exposing the forms of barbarism inherent in modern capitalist civilization, could have written about this 'biogenocide' resulting from AIDS (if he had not died from it himself). He would have undoubtedly seen in it a particularly revolting manifestation of 'biopower', the power created in the nineteenth century by adding the 'right to make live and to let die' to the 'sovereignty's old right – to take life or let live'.[25] Today this 'biopower' too has been 'globalized'. 'Let die' – isn't this what the West is guilty of toward people with AIDS, and with many other plagues that are decimating the world's poorest peoples? What other conclusion is possible when a fraction of the richest countries' military budgets and other superfluous spending would be enough to throttle or eradicate these diseases, not to mention save the lives of those already infected? Doesn't 'biogenocide' through failure to assist bear the same relation to genocide through extermination that 'to let die' does to the old power to 'take life'?

> How can this state, whose objective is essentially to foster life, let people die? How are the power of death and the function of death exercised in a political system centred on biopower? Given that this power's objective is essentially to make live, how can it let die? How can the power of death, the function of death, be exercised in a political system centred upon biopower?
>
> It is, I think, at this point that racism intervenes ... It is indeed the emergence of this biopower that inscribes it in the mechanisms of the State. It is at this moment that racism is inscribed as a basic mechanism of power, as it is exercised in modern States. As a result, the modern State can scarcely function without becoming involved with racism at some point, with certain limits and subject to certain conditions.
>
> What in fact is racism? It is primarily a way of introducing a break into the domain of life that is under power's control: the break between what must live and what must die.[26]

Rather than a 'clash of civilizations', the battle in progress is thus definitely a clash of the barbarisms that civilizations secrete in varying quantities in the course of the long historical and dialectical process of Civilization. The more gluttonous societies are, the greater the barbarism they excrete. Today these various barbarisms threaten once more to swallow the most essential achievements of Civilization in the maw of a generalized Barbarism – for at moments of crisis the specific modalities in which the potential for Barbarism finds expression can always win out over Civilization. Nazi barbarism, produced by a country at the summit of advanced 'Western civilization', is an instance of this. Enzo Traverso reaffirmed this lesson in the conclusion to his book, which Hannah Arendt, the author of *The Origins of Totalitarianism* and its inspirer, would not have disowned.[27] We have clearly arrived once more at one of those epochal moments at which, as Freud explained, the drive toward death and destruction – until then kept under control by Civilization in the service of the life force Eros – frees itself of all inhibitions:

> In circumstances that are favorable to it, when the mental counter-forces which ordinarily inhibit it are out of action, [aggressiveness] also manifests itself spontaneously and reveals man as a savage beast to whom consideration toward his own kind is something alien. Anyone who calls to mind the atrocities committed during the racial migrations or the invasions of the Huns, or by the people known as Mongols under Genghis Khan and Tamerlane, or even, indeed, the horrors of the recent World War – anyone who calls these things to mind will have to bow humbly before the truth of this view.[28]

The admirers of the 11 September bombers cheered at the spectacle of the Twin Towers collapsing and call for more. The admirers of the US military found the spectacle of the crushing of Afghanistan delectable, and call for more. We are clearly in one of those 'times of social upheaval' in which, according to Elias, 'cruelty and joy in destruction and torment of others, like proof of physical superiority, ... break out more directly, uninhibitedly, less impeded by shame and repugnance.'[29]

On both sides, 'absolute hostility' toward the 'absolute enemy', to use Carl Schmitt's words, thus entails the deployment of extreme violence and a logic of extermination: 'People who use such means against other people find themselves constrained to destroy these other people, who are their victims as well as their objects, morally as well. They are forced to declare the entire enemy camp criminal and inhuman, to reduce it to a complete nullity. Otherwise they would be criminals and monsters themselves.'[30]

Taken separately, each barbarous act can be judged equally reprehensible from a moral standpoint. No civilized ethic can justify deliberate assassination of non-combatants or children, whether indiscriminate or deliberate, by state or non-governmental terror. There is an international consensus condemning the intentional murder of civilians in order to spread terror. Murdering civilians should be just as reprehensible when it is an ineluctable consequence, known in advance, of an attack on combatants that is not required as a matter of imperative necessity. The notion of 'collateral damage' applied by the Pentagon to civilian victims of its bombings not only cynically reduces the murder of innocents to something banal; it is a hypocritical attempt to excuse the murders that result from repetitive recourse to military force. When there is any possible alternative to such attacks, and when they destroy more human lives than they save, such attacks are simply criminal.

Nevertheless, from the point of view of basic fairness, we cannot wrap ourselves in a metaphysical ethic that rejects all forms of barbarism equally. The different barbarisms do not carry the same weight in the scales of justice. Admittedly, barbarism can never be an instrument of 'legitimate self-defence'; it is always illegitimate by definition. But this does not change the fact that when two barbarisms clash, the stronger, the one that acts as the oppressor, is still the more culpable.[31] Except in cases of manifest irrationality, the barbarism of the weak is most often, logically enough, a reaction to the barbarism of the strong. Otherwise why would the weak provoke the strong, at the risk of being crushed themselves? This is, incidentally, why the strong seek to hide their culpability by portraying their adversaries as demented, demonic and bestial.

*Preventing Terrorism*

If the objective is truly to put an end to Barbarism, to all barbarisms, then the fundamental causes of barbarities must be eliminated. What, then, are the causes of the rise of barbarisms on a world scale? Let us look first at the international clash between the barbarities inherently pertaining to different civilizations, beginning with the barbarism of the weak. We start from the logical hypothesis that the barbarism of the weak is an epiphenomenon of the barbarism of the strong, and therefore has its origins in the barbarism of the strong. Let us begin at the beginning, the starting point of this book, namely the barbarism that resulted in the horrendous mass murder of 11 September 2001.

How can we explain the inexorable escalation in al-Qaʻida's level of violence to more and more destructive forms of terrorism, without falling back on madness or absolute evil in Hannah Arendt's sense – 'absolute because it can no longer be deduced from humanly comprehensible motives'?[32] The people in Washington knew the answer and understood it perfectly, far in advance. It is at the heart of the concept of 'asymmetric means' mentioned above. This concept appeared in Washington's official publications, referring to the conflict between the United States and bin Laden's network, even before the conflict reached a new peak in 1998, when US embassies were attacked in East Africa and US cruise missiles were launched against Afghanistan and Sudan.

The first quadrennial report on US defence – published in 1997 in accordance with the 1996 National Defense Authorization Act, which required each new administration to present its vision of military planning to Congress – explained the new propensity to resort to 'asymmetric means' very well, with remarkable prescience about what was in store for the United States:

> Indeed, US dominance in the conventional military arena may encourage adversaries to use such asymmetric means [unconventional means of attack, such as terrorism] to attack our forces and interests overseas and Americans at home. That is, they are likely to seek advantage over the United States by

using unconventional approaches to *circumvent* or *undermine* our strengths while *exploiting* our vulnerabilities. Strategically, an aggressor may seek to avoid direct military confrontation with the United States, using instead means such as terrorism, NBC [nuclear, biological and chemical] threats, information warfare, or environmental sabotage to achieve its goals.[33]

This document shows incontrovertibly that even if the techniques used on 11 September caught the US government by surprise, the bare fact that a large-scale terrorist attack occurred on US soil was in no sense a surprise for it. All the post-11 September rhetoric about the sudden end of US invulnerability and the vanished safety of US territory is presumably meant for consumption by the unwitting public. In reality, the appropriate authorities had given up this invulnerability for lost quite a while before. Several actions had already undermined it in practice, including the first attempt, which we must not forget, to destroy the World Trade Center towers in 1993. This first attempt was not foiled by the vigilance and efficiency of the agencies charged with protecting the United States from attack; it failed only because the mixture of explosives used was not powerful enough. If the attack had succeeded it would have taken many more lives than the attacks that happened eight and a half years later.[34]

In the face of adversaries this determined – and prepared to commit suicide – clearly no preventative security measures could ever be enough. The billions of dollars that the Bush Administration is now spending on 'homeland security' will not accomplish much – except considerably strengthening the Big Brother watching over the words and deeds of US citizens themselves.[35]

The determination of the US enemies and their 'absolute hostility' make deterrence an irrelevant notion: 'The deterrence concept requires that there be both conflict and common interest between the parties involved; it is as inapplicable to a situation of pure and complete antagonism of interest as it is to the case of pure and complete common interest.'[36]

It is therefore necessary to rely on political prevention. In other words, the causes of 'absolute hostility' must be reduced or eliminated, in such a way that a 'common interest' emerges as a possibility. How did the US government try to prevent the catastrophe foretold? Bill Clinton's first inauguration was greeted, after all, by the first attempt to destroy Manhattan's twin towers. Each of his two successive administrations – the second one (1997–2001) in particular, after the threats were made more explicit and the conflict with the al-Qa'ida network had continued to escalate – viewed this prospect with anxiety.

The first question that we need to ask in this respect is: given the high price in human lives that the United States has paid on several occasions for keeping its troops on the Saudi kingdom's soil, why hasn't Washington pulled them out? There are only about five thousand US troops stationed there, after all. They could have been stationed from the beginning in neighbouring Kuwait, where their presence would have caused many fewer problems. From the moment of their arrival in the kingdom in 1990, the US troops were notorious for the strong hostile reactions they elicited from the population. Washington knew full well how many long-term problems stationing troops there would cause; this is why US forces had had to evacuate the US base at Dhahran in 1962, as we have already mentioned. Successive US administrations' stubborn determination to keep these five thousand troops in place, as proof of its tutelary protection of this Islamic Texas, has been a choice made despite the risks involved for the safety of US citizens. US citizens have already paid for those five thousand troops with almost as many deaths.

The second component of the political prevention of anti-US terrorism of Islamic origin relates to US policy toward Iraq. Over the years, against the wishes of some of its own allies and partners, the United States kept the deadly embargo in place. Far from inconveniencing the tyrant who ruled Iraq by means of terror, the embargo made things easier for Saddam Hussein by debilitating the Iraqi people, by now an object of indignant commiseration throughout the Arab world. This attitude has contributed substantially to increasing anti-US feelings in this part of the world, allowing bin Laden to assume the position of recognized spokesperson for the most vehement expression of these feelings.

The third component of the political prevention of anti-US terrorism of Islamic origin relates to US policy toward Israel and Palestine. This is the only field in which the Clinton Administration actually tried to do something. Inadequate as its attempt was, its preventive political activity in this field can be seen in hindsight as a model of farsightedness compared with the Bush Administration's attitude before and after 11 September:

> Clinton's overarching priority in the Middle East, and the animating foreign policy goal of his presidency, was peace between Israel and its neighbors. Martin Indyk, who advised him at the White House and as assistant secretary of state for Near Eastern affairs, described terrorism's inverse relationship to success at the bargaining table.
>
> 'After the Gulf War and the collapse of the Soviet Union, there was a very real sense of a window of opportunity to achieve a comprehensive peace in the Middle East,' he said. 'That became the priority. The assumption was that if you could achieve that kind of breakthrough, it would have a transforming effect on the whole region.' That, in turn, would 'deal a blow to those who opposed the peace process, particularly using terrorism to do so.'[37]

So the Clinton Administration saw a close connection between the propensity toward 'terrorism' and the unfolding Israeli-Arab conflict. This connection is as obvious as the relationship between Israel's 1982 invasion of Lebanon and the first suicide bombings directed at the United States in this same country in 1983. According to Martin Indyk, this insight helps explain the priority that the Clinton Administration gave to the attempt to reach a Middle East settlement. The fact remains that the administration did not intervene in a balanced way, but rather showed a clear bias in Israel's favour.

Although no credible, lasting peace is possible in this part of the world, which exports violence to the rest of the world, without Israeli concessions, the Clinton Administration failed to pressure its

Israeli ally strongly to make them. Instead it joined successive Israeli governments in trying to extract even more concessions from the Palestinian leadership – concessions of a kind that the Palestinian people would have inevitably rejected and which would have undermined a new accord from the start. The US attitude reinforced an interpretation of the 13 September 1993 Washington accords (the interpretation most detrimental to Palestinian interests) that contributed to the tragic way the Israeli-Palestinian 'peace process' became bogged down.

Yet the attitude of George W. Bush's Administration was even worse than its predecessor's. The new president thought he could demonstrate his political shrewdness by refusing to 'substitute' for the parties to the conflict and making a show of 'benign neglect' in face of bloody events in the Middle East. This was all the more disastrous given that Ariel Sharon, one of the Zionist right's most brutal and extremist figures, had come to power in February 2001 after having deliberately provoked an explosion of Palestinian rage with his untimely appearance on the esplanade of the Jerusalem mosques on 28 September 2000.

This date marks the start of the 'second Intifada' and its brutal repression. Bin Laden accordingly put more emphasis on solidarity with the Palestinians in the run-up to the 11 September attacks a year later. From June 2001 on he had a two-hour videotape distributed in which he boasted of US vulnerability, shown by the suicide bombing of the destroyer USS *Cole* in October 2000, and called on Muslims to redouble their efforts to strike new blows at the US. The edition of the *New York Times* for 9 September 2001, two days before the catastrophe that would strike its native city, devoted a long article to this videotape. It is worth reprinting a few passages from this article:

> Mr bin Laden uses the tape to spell out a continuing nightmare for his principal enemies, the United States and Israel. He promises an intensified holy war that includes aid to Palestinians fighting Israel – an important shift in emphasis, according to intelligence analysts. In recent years, through a series of violent attacks, Mr bin Laden's main focus has been on

driving American forces from the Arabian peninsula ...

Much of the tape focuses on the current upheaval in Israel and the Palestinian territories. What is not clear, say intelligence experts, is whether Mr bin Laden plans to mount direct attacks on Israeli targets, or whether he is firing followers' passions for attacks elsewhere. 'Our brothers in Palestine are waiting for you anxiously, and expect you to strike at America and Israel,' Mr bin Laden says. 'God's earth is wide and their interests are everywhere.' ...

Vincent Cannistraro, former head of counterterrorist operations for the Central Intelligence Agency, who reviewed the tape, said Mr bin Laden's warnings of new attacks should be taken seriously. 'The intifada has clearly focused his attention on the Palestinian problem, which he sees in holy war terms – the Palestinians being oppressed by the Israelis, in ways that are only possible because of the support they get from the United States,' he said.

'This has reinforced his opinion about the United States and its policies in the whole of the Middle East. It sharpens his instincts for attack.'[38]

This article allows us to judge the US government's share of responsibility in the disaster that was about to hit the country. Yet the US people have not brought this responsibility home to their government. On the contrary, they have even given the government's most responsible individual, George W. Bush, a record-high approval rating in the polls. This shows the extent of the media onslaught to which it has been subjected, both in the forms described in chapter 1 of this book and in the way the information laid out above has been kept from US public opinion.

Given the scale of the catastrophe that the Bush Administration did nothing to prevent, its culpable negligence would have been more than enough to provoke the immediate resignation of any honest, responsible leader. But the very way the forty-third president made his way to the White House, not to speak of the Enron scandal and other events since the elections, showed that Bush is neither honest nor responsible. It is enough to make one marvel at the fact that Bill Clinton's lies in the Lewinsky affair almost drove him to resign or led to his impeachment. The surge in George W. Bush's popularity after 11 September shows that the event's true lessons are still far from having been learned. Indeed, it shows that people in the US have drawn conclusions that are the exact opposite of the right ones.

So far we have mentioned three factors to explain the origins of the political-religious terrorism targeting the United States: the presence of US troops in the Saudi kingdom, the Iraq embargo, and the Israeli-Palestinian conflict. We will not dwell further on the way in which the Bush Administration deals with these Middle East issues. It is clear enough that it has done nothing until now but throw more oil on the fire, forgetting once more that the United States itself falls within the perimeter of this conflagration.

## On Asymmetric Dominance

Even more fundamental is the overall strategic vision that underlies Washington's Middle East policies. These policies are only one illustration among others of a general attitude focused on preserving US 'dominance'. According to the Pentagon's own analysis, this is what explains the increasing tendency of Washington's adversaries to resort to 'asymmetric means', targeting both US missions abroad and US civilians at home. US 'dominance', Washington's euphemism for domination, is at the heart of post-Cold War US military planning, as designed during Clinton's two terms in office and defined in two strategic documents: the 1996 *Joint Vision 2010* and the 1997 Quadrennial Defense Review.

The importance of the paradigm shift implied by substituting the notion of 'dominance' for the notion of 'defense', which gives the DOD (Department of Defense) a new mission without even requiring it to change its acronym, can hardly be overestimated. The collapse of the Soviet Union and the end of the bipolar world have radically reshaped the world strategic landscape. It has disposed of the United States' concern with containing its global adversary, conceived in terms of a priority for defence. The chief meaning of deterrence itself could therefore change: instead of deterring adversaries from acting, it now means deterring adversaries from *re*acting. In other words, deterrence must now assure the United States, to an unprecedented degree and extent, the 'freedom of action' that is the supreme objective of classical strategic thinking.[39]

Unipolar military domination by the United States, established on the ruins of the USSR, presented Washington with a strong temptation to consolidate it and make it permanent, as the hard core of a historically unprecedented, global political hegemony. The US government could not resist the temptation, the drunkenness of hubris, despite the warnings made by its wisest officials.[40] The US sole concern has become to assure itself 'full spectrum dominance', that is, dominance in all types of conflict, 'to ensure we are persuasive in peace, decisive in war, and preeminent in any form of conflict.'[41] In other words, the United States must be master of the world.

This 'dominance' itself is based on a major asymmetry in the existing military forces and capacities in the world in the United States' favour. Its main operational concept is the 'dominant maneuver': a multi-dimensional control of the battle space that 'will provide US forces with overwhelming and asymmetric advantages to accomplish assigned operational tasks.'[42] The new Quadrennial Defense Review, presented to Congress by current Pentagon boss Donald Rumsfeld a few days after the 11 September attacks, emphasizes the United States' asymmetric advantage even more strongly. This 2001 report innovates by replacing the 'threat-based strategy' prevalent in earlier doctrines with a 'capabilities-based strategy'. In other words, US military readiness is now no longer supposed to be based on an estimate of military means in the hands of identified potential enemies, but on a summation of all the military means that could be used by any hypothetical adversary whatsoever.

As the secretary of defense explains in his introduction:

> Adopting this capabilities-based approach to planning requires that the nation maintain its military advantages in key areas

> while it develops new areas of military advantage and denies
> asymmetric advantages to adversaries ... In short, it requires
> the transformation of US forces, capabilities, and institutions
> to extend America's asymmetric advantages well into the
> future.[43]

In the last decade of the twentieth century, the first decade of
the post-Cold War period, the US armed forces were required to
maintain a level of readiness sufficient to wage two major theatre wars
simultaneously. At the same time they had to be able to carry out a
range of other operations assigned to them, from more limited wars
to 'peacekeeping' operations. The two 'major theatre wars' referred to,
without naming them explicitly, the United States' two main potential
adversaries, China and Russia.

In the initial period, however, these high demands put on military
planning were still compatible with a cut in military spending from the
record levels reached under Ronald Reagan. The phenomenal decline
in Russian military might from the level of the ex-USSR made this
possible, while concerns about reducing the colossal budget deficit of
earlier years made it desirable. The US military budget then stabilized
in the mid-1990s at a level still worthy of the Cold War years: one-
third of world military spending, and equivalent to the combined
military budgets of the six next highest-spending countries: not only
Russia and China, but also Japan, France, Germany and the United
Kingdom.[44]

A new upward trend began in February 1999, in the run-up to
the Kosovo war. This took place under the Clinton Administration;
though the Bush Administration's responsibility for the current
situation is unlikely to be overlooked, the Clinton Administration's
responsibility for the present state of things should also not be
forgotten.[45] The Pentagon proudly announced 'the first sustained long-
term increase in defense funding since the end of the Cold War' ($112
billion through 2005). At the same time Defense Secretary William
Cohen declared that Washington would demand amendments to
the ABM (anti-ballistic missile) treaty signed with Moscow in 1972
so that the United States could go ahead with its National Missile

Defense project. If Moscow did not go along, Cohen announced at that early date, the United States would abrogate the ABM treaty unilaterally.

Under the impact of 11 September, George W. Bush's Administration would push these tendencies, well under way under its predecessor, to the limit. The scenario of two major theatre wars was revised somewhat in the new military plans, in the direction of a stronger commitment to full spectrum dominance:

> The United States is not abandoning planning for two conflicts to plan for fewer than two. On the contrary, DOD is changing the concept altogether by planning for victory across the spectrum of possible conflict ...
>
> At the direction of the President, US forces will be capable of decisively defeating an adversary in one of the two theaters in which US forces are conducting major combat operations by imposing America's will and removing any future threat it could pose. This capability will include the ability to occupy territory or set the conditions for a regime change if so directed.[46]

Carried away by its own more-patriotic-than-thou rhetoric, the Bush Administration submitted a military budget to Congress that included the biggest one-year military spending increase since Reagan's first budget twenty years before. It proposed an increase of $48 billion, bringing total military spending to $379 billion. This increase equalled the whole of Japan's military budget, or even the estimated real military budget of Russia. It raised total US military spending planned for fiscal 2002–3 to a sum equivalent to the combined military budgets of the fifteen next biggest military powers, to more than double the combined military spending of the European member states of the European Union and NATO – and to the whole of Russia's gross domestic product![47]

This new display of military prodigality was accompanied by an unprecedented outbreak of arrogance and hubris in US foreign policy. The United States deployed a whole range of practices that trampled international law, international treaties and international public opinion underfoot. Admittedly, US unilateralism did not begin with George W. Bush – far from it.[48] But under his administration it has reached a level where the forms it takes and the heights it reaches are exasperating Washington's closest allies.[49]

## Hegemonic Unilateralism

Even the way Bush reacted to the 11 September attacks was a glaring illustration of the hegemonic unilateralism that now characterizes US policies more than ever before.[50] We must note first of all the quintessentially imperial arrogance with which Washington demanded that the Kabul government hand over Osama bin Laden immediately, when he was still only suspected of having played a role in the attacks. Any government that respected the procedures of international law and refused to accede to the kind of 'rendition' practised by governments under the US thumb[51] would have demanded that the United States submit a legally and formally adequate extradition request before it made its decision. Washington's European allies were put in the awkward position of having to refuse to extradite suspects demanded by their transatlantic 'godfather', given that the United States gave no guarantees that they would receive a fair trial, that it planned to try defendants in military courts, and that it continues to apply the death penalty – all conditions incompatible with extradition under European law.[52]

The Taliban regime asked only that the United States give it evidence of bin Laden's involvement in 11 September. Washington's sole answer was to issue an ultimatum: Give us bin Laden or we bomb you.[53] In less than a month after the attacks, US troops began to pour into Afghanistan, devastating the already wretched country, crushing it under military hardware and setting it on fire. Along the way the United States killed a large number of Afghan civilians,[54] who were no more responsible for 11 September than Iraqi children are for Saddam Hussein's megalomaniacal activities. But Bush Administration officials seem less likely to choke on remorse for this 'collateral damage' than their president is to choke on a pretzel. According to Walzer this was undoubtedly a 'just war' because it was 'preventive' (as all Israeli military actions are supposed to be, too). The US could not take the risk of trying to prosecute the terrorists in court, Walzer said – because there might not be enough evidence![55]

No other country in the world not bordering on Afghanistan would have had the means to act as the United States did. If 11 September had happened on some other country's soil, the country's only recourse would have been the one foreseen in international law, the UN Security Council. This option was also available to Washington. Unlike in Kosovo and even more than against Iraq in 1990, Russia and China were ready to back a US war against the Taliban, since in this case their interests converged with US interests. The Security Council even explicitly offered Bush its services. In its resolution 1368, adopted on 12 September 2001, the UN expressed 'its readiness to take all necessary steps to respond to the terrorist attacks of 11 September 2001, and to combat all forms of terrorism, in accordance with its responsibilities under the Charter of the United Nations.'[56]

It would thus have been possible to act in the framework of chapter VII of the UN Charter. The Security Council, noting that an 'act of aggression' had taken place qualifying as a crime against humanity, could have invited the Kabul government to bring the defendants before an international tribunal created specially for that purpose, on the model of the already existing international criminal tribunals.[57] This solution would certainly not have ensured equal justice, but rather one-sided, biased justice, as is the case with the international criminal tribunal dealing with the wars in ex-Yugoslavia. But it would have been infinitely more 'just' and more legitimate than the military courts set up by the Bush Administration, not to mention the order to get hold of bin Laden 'dead or alive'. If the Kabul government in cooperation with bin Laden had refused to carry out the resolution, the Security Council could have taken the measures of graduated escalation foreseen in articles 41 and 42 of chapter VII of the UN Charter, up to and including 'the use of armed force.'[58]

George W. Bush could even have waged 'his' war, as or almost as he wanted to, within the UN framework. After all this is what his father had done against Iraq – a war waged in the UN's name but not by the UN, as UN Secretary General Javier Pérez de Cuellar rightly remarked at the time. True, Bush Senior needed the world organization's endorsement in order to convince Congress to give him a green light for his war against Saddam Hussein. Bush Junior needed no such thing. By September both houses of Congress had adopted – unanimously, minus the single vote of courageous California Democratic Representative Barbara Lee – an 'Authorization for Use of Military Force' under the 1973 War Powers Resolution.

Even without acting in the framework of international law and the UN Charter, Washington could still have resorted to a multilateral variant of unilateralism by waging the war in the framework of NATO, as it had in the preceding Kosovo war. The Atlantic Alliance's very obliging secretary general, George Robertson, prompted it to react as early as 12 September. For the first time in its history NATO invoked article 5 of its founding treaty, referring to collective self-defence of its member states. But the Pentagon had found its experience of collegial military management in the Balkans out of keeping with its professional traditions, and had sworn that it would never go through that again.

The US hyperpower's hegemonic unilateralism has been well expressed in two political axioms. Formulated in the aftermath of 11 September, they constitute the essence of the new administration's doctrine. George W. Bush pronounced the first himself in his 20 September speech to Congress, speaking to all the nations of the world. It is his now famous 'Either you are with us, or you are with the terrorists',[59] which enjoined every government on the planet to ally with Washington under pain of being treated like the Taliban. Its Manichean, anathematizing logic criminalizes any attempt to maintain some distance from both the Taliban and the United States, any refusal by states opposing terrorism to align with Washington. Defense Secretary Donald Rumsfeld set forth the second axiom three days later on CBS, when he announced peremptorily that 'the mission determines the coalition, and we don't allow coalitions to determine the mission.'[60] And, of course, Washington gets to determine the mission. George W. Bush confirmed this in his 29 January 2002 State of the Union speech, when he designated Iraq, Iran and North

Korea, along with organizations labelled 'terrorist' by Washington, as forming an 'axis of evil'.

Bush has announced that this 'war on terror' will have to last several more years. In this war the United States alone will choose the targets. It will assign to its allies the tasks that it wants them to take on, under US command or supervision: essentially the tasks that the Pentagon balks at taking on itself. Afghanistan, where the United States used the Northern Alliance's troops as auxiliary forces for the ground offensive, provides a good illustration. The Northern Alliance was an indispensable factor in evicting Mullah Omar's Taliban, complementing the more than overwhelming superiority provided by the US capacity to strike from a distance.

Then, once the Taliban were got rid of, Washington called on its NATO auxiliaries to take on alone the risks of patrolling in Afghan cities. Here was one of those 'nation-building' missions that Bush had said during his presidential campaign were unworthy of the US armed forces. This applies all the more, of course, when the mission is considered impossible, in a country ruled by warlords engaged in bloody factional and ethnic rivalries. The NATO auxiliary forces were deployed under the aegis of the United Nations, as in the Balkans. Washington thus killed two birds with one stone, reintroducing two organizations that had been frustrated at being shut out from the war against the Taliban.

For the third time, therefore, following the Gulf war and Kosovo war, Washington has demonstrated the purely utilitarian relationship that it maintains with the UN. Franklin D. Roosevelt once conceived the organization as a framework for managing international relations under the rule of law and settling conflicts peacefully, and as the only body authorized to confer legitimacy to the use of force in international affairs. But in the post-Cold War period, in the eyes of today's US presidents, the UN is nothing more than a post-war management tool for territories ravaged by military interventions decided in Washington.

The United States can get away with this kind of behaviour, placing itself above international law and international institutions, thanks precisely to its military dominance over the rest of the world. It is working incessantly to strengthen this dominance, widening each year the gulf that separates its military capabilities from those of the rest of the world. It combines this asymmetric power of the strong over the weak with the example it sets by breaking all the rules and laws. In other words, it is inflicting the reign of its overpowering, arbitrary will on the rest of the world. This is the most effective recipe for making countless people reach the conclusion that the United States' 'asymmetric advantages' can only by countered by 'asymmetric means' targeting the most vulnerable among the US population, and accordingly turn to terrorism.

The US government itself, through the political and military choices it has made since the end of the Cold War, is inexorably producing the terrorism that it means to fight against. Bush's 'war on terror' will inevitably lead to new terrorist attacks on US citizens. These attacks risk attaining much more murderous proportions than on 11 September 2001, and can originate in a greater and greater range of regions as Washington extends the geographical scope of its military interventions in the name of that same 'war on terror'. According to FBI experts testifying before the Senate in December 2001, capturing or killing bin Laden would affect only 40 to 50 percent of the al-Qa'ida network's activities. Al-Qa'ida has hundreds of members still at large who are capable of organizing sophisticated attacks, not to speak of thousands of members of allied organizations and a potential recruitment base estimated at several tens of thousands.[61]

Rumsfeld's Deputy Defense Secretary Paul Wolfowitz recently said at the 38th Munich International Conference on Security Policy, 'What happened on September 11, as terrible as it was, is but a pale shadow of what will happen if terrorists use weapons of mass destruction.' He added, 'Our approach has to aim at prevention and not merely punishment.' Anyone tempted to take hope at this sensible-sounding sentence needs to think again; Wolfowitz's conception of 'preventing' terrorism deserves an honoured place in the annals of repressive self-deception. He made his meaning clear in his subsequent remarks: 'Self-defense requires prevention and sometimes preemption. It is not possible to defend against every threat, in every place, at every conceivable time. The only defense against terrorism is to take war to the enemy.'[62]

According to Washington's own analysis, therefore, it can only respond to attacks by 'asymmetric means' provoked by its military dominance by increasing the asymmetry of its dominance still further and extending the areas in which it is exercised, in the name of 'preemption'. In so doing it is bound to provoke new asymmetric attacks on its troops and civilian population. This determination to increase the United States' 'asymmetric advantages' is thus inexorably confirming a configuration of the world in which the 'hyperpower' brings the hatred of all other 'civilizations' down on its head.[63] It is even earning the antipathy of its own Western allies, or, in Zbigniew Brzezinski's Machiavellian formula, its 'vassals', by virtue of 'security dependence'.[64]

Several months before 11 September one US commentator responded in advance to the Bush Administration's current 'preventive' logic:

> Can we do anything to prevent terrorist attacks? Not really. Oh, we can probably raise the costs and make it more difficult. Better intelligence analysis and coordination might help, as would hardening targets (though the USS *Cole* was as hardened as it was going to get). We also could raise the stakes by instituting a policy stating that terrorist strikes against American forces or the homeland will provoke a declaration of war against those who use or sponsor it.
>
> But if someone really is willing to meet their maker in order to attack you, chances are they will succeed. In short, if you want to be [*sic*] a global hegemony you have to be prepared to pay the price.[65]

Nor would there be much point in transforming the United States into the continental equivalent of a 'gated community': a residential area for the paranoid wealthy, protected by private guards and electronic surveillance systems. Zbigniew Brzezinski himself has described the meaning of the National Missile Defense project in these terms.[66] The real, inescapable question is this: is the US population really ready to endure even more September 11ths, as the unavoidable price of a global hegemony that only benefits its ruling class? It needs to think about this, and fast.

## Apocalyptic Terrorism

The rising tide of barbarisms goes far beyond the consequences of US military and political 'dominance' and the international clash among barbarities inherent in different civilizations. The rise of barbarisms directed against their own societies is just as important, whether they are governmental, capitalist, politically extremist or fanatically religious barbarisms, or even barbarisms verging on lunacy. Let us begin with the ones that are emerging within 'civil society'. In the world's poorest societies these phenomena are far from new. But they are also spreading in a striking way in the richest societies, which are supposed to have come furthest on the road to Civilization and pacific mores.

Two individuals have come to symbolize the rising trend toward mass murder within the most developed countries: US right-wing extremist Timothy McVeigh and Japanese guru Shoko Asahara of the sect Aum Shinrikyo (Aum Supreme Truth). Compared to them bin Laden seems like a model of political rationality.

McVeigh, together with an accomplice, was responsible for blowing up the Oklahoma City Federal Building with a chemical fertilizer bomb on 19 April 1995, killing 168 people and wounding several hundred others. They belonged to the US Nazi-like extreme right, which ranges from the old Ku Klux Klan to the Aryan Nations by way of the 'patriotic' militia movement. Put together, all these organizations represent a sizeable body of people. But apparently McVeigh and his accomplice acted on their own, inspired by a novel written by a neo-Nazi, in which they had even found the recipe for their bomb. The book's hero, a 'patriot', fights to free the US from its government, an illegitimate regime controlled by an international Jewish conspiracy. The novel ends with a nuclear explosion and the triumph of the elite of the 'white race', after Jews and non-whites have been exterminated on a planetary scale in order to save the world.

As for Asahara, he led an organization of several thousand people from various social backgrounds, with followers in several countries. The Aum Shinrikyo sect's methods of recruitment and indoctrination were similar to those of apocalyptic religious sects, including brainwashing and coercion. It had quite a few high-level scientists among its members and substantial financial resources (more than a billion dollars according to some estimates). It was thus able to create a network of laboratories and spend large amounts of money perfecting various formulas for mass murder (including $30 million spent on chemical weapons). Haunted by Hiroshima, Asahara announced that the end of the world was at hand; it would take the form of a third world war and a nuclear holocaust, which only the members of his sect would survive.

He thought he could hasten the coming of this apocalypse by using weapons of mass destruction. After having explored the whole gamut of possibilities and failing to acquire a nuclear bomb, Aum Shinrikyo used biological and chemical weapons – several times, in fact. Leaving aside the targeted attacks, like the unsuccessful attacks on the Japanese parliament, the imperial family, and the Matsumoto judges, we need only consider this sect's attempts at indiscriminate mass murder, beginning with biological weapons. The sect accumulated a frightening stockpile of bioweapons of various kinds; it even tried to obtain specimens of the Ebola virus. It tried, again unsuccessfully, to spray spores of the now infamous anthrax bacillus from the roof of a Tokyo apartment building in June 1993. In March 1995 an attempt to spray botulin in the Tokyo subway also failed.

Unfortunately, the sect's attacks with chemical weapons were more effective – it had also acquired a whole stockpile of chemical weapons – in particular the ones carried out with sarin gas. The most serious was its second attack in the Tokyo subway on 20 March 1995, five days after its abortive bioterrorist attack. Five sect members spread sarin gas solution in five different subway cars. Since they had not yet perfected their technique, they killed fewer people than they could have with the amount of gas they used. Still, there were twelve deaths and five thousand people affected physically or psychologically. This attack finally led to the dismantling of Aum Shinrikyo (whose immunity year after year until then bore a certain resemblance to that of the Yakuza, the Japanese mafia).

Do these two cases also constitute exceptions, which prove the rule that 'everything is for the best in the best of all possible worlds'? Must we accept Fukuyama's verdict after 11 September that 'modernity is a very powerful freight train that will not be derailed by recent events, however painful and unprecedented'?[67]

The US psychopathic-leaning far right and the Aum Shinrikyo sect are social phenomena in themselves, involving thousands upon thousands of people. While the Tokyo subway attack and the Oklahoma City bombing turned into setbacks for both of them, the setbacks are only specific and temporary.[68] Moreover, they are but two avatars of a much more widespread phenomenon on a world scale, one on which we have no reliable estimates. All forms of terrorism and mass murder carried out by groups against the societies that they themselves emerge from are part of this same phenomenon. It needs to be distinguished from transnational forms of mass terrorism. The 11 September attacks belong to the latter category, while the murderous actions of the Algerian Armed Islamic Group (GIA) fall under the former. Both of them are different from Cold War-era forms of terrorism, whether political, nationalist, revolutionary or counter-revolutionary, which rarely aimed at mass murder.

The number of victims of these two categories combined shows a clearly rising curve over the past two decades, as all studies of the subject agree. The number of attacks increased spectacularly – a tally of major terrorist incidents occurring between 1961 and 2001, prepared by the historical division of the US State Department,[69] records a total of fifteen during the two decades from 1961 to 1980, then thirty-four in the single decade 1981–90, and eighty in 1991–2000. The attacks' 'lethality', the number of deaths caused, has also skyrocketed. A list of terrorist attacks in the twentieth century causing more than a hundred deaths includes only three in the century's first seven decades. Then, beginning in the 1980s, nine attacks are recorded up until 1995, going from the suicide bombing against the US troops in Lebanon in 1983 to the Oklahoma City bombing.[70] The list was drawn up before the 1998 attack on the US embassy in Nairobi, Kenya, which caused 291 deaths and more than five thousand injuries.

On the United States' own territory the increase in the attacks' lethality is striking. During the 1980s 267 different attacks killed a total of 23 people. In the following decade there were only 60 attacks, but the Oklahoma City bombing alone caused 168 deaths, bringing the decade's total to 182.[71] With 11 September 2001, the first decade of the twenty-first century has already beaten all the records. A few days later the United States, following Japan, experienced its first attempted terrorist acts with so-called weapons of mass destruction: the wave of anthrax attacks that began in early October 2001. Only the inadequacy of the method of dissemination used and the uneven quality of the spores kept down the number of victims that these attacks claimed. As these lines are written the perpetrators of the attacks have still not been discovered: all the evidence suggests that they are native to the United States, not 'transnational' terrorists.

Biological weapons provide incomparably greater possibilities for killing and terrorizing people than chemical weapons[72] – a potential that could never be matched by the murderous ingenuity that transformed regular airliners into giant incendiary missiles, with box-cutter knives as its only weapons. This potential is increased substantially by what Foucault called 'an excess of biopower', which puts it 'beyond all human sovereignty' and 'appears when it becomes technologically and politically possible for man not only to manage life but to make it proliferate, to create living matter, to build the monster, and, ultimately, to build viruses that cannot be controlled and that are universally destructive.'[73] Uncontrolled, unregulated development of biogenetics and genetic manipulation, in a world where making profits is considered the highest good, not only multiplies the risks of unintended catastrophes but also heralds even worse catastrophes brought about deliberately for terrorist purposes.

It is possible by means of genetic manipulation to increase considerably the characteristic that gives biological weapons their fearsome superiority: they are the only weapons capable of ensuring their own 'proliferation' once they have been set loose in a favourable environment. Disseminating biological substances requires neither sophisticated means nor enormous ingenuity. Since they act by being inhaled or ingested, they can be sprayed using an airborne device over a large area or by an atomizer in an enclosed space. Depending on their nature, they can also be introduced into drinking water supplies or food products. A successful operation could cause hundreds of thousands of deaths using a mass of organisms weighing between a few pounds and a couple of hundred pounds.

In addition, biological weapons are relatively easy to produce. In the case of several kinds of biological cultures a rudimentary laboratory in a bathroom with a bathtub is enough. These weapons can also be transported without being detected, including across frontiers, either in initial doses that can be cultivated so as to produce the desired quantities or even in quantities that are already big enough to fill a whole cemetery.

Nuclear weapons are rather more difficult to obtain or make. But they can be quite effectively replaced by much more accessible radiological bombs. A Russian military expert described these bombs as follows:

> Such a weapon is, in essence, a device designed to inflict a deadly and massive dose of radioactive contamination on a large area without a nuclear explosion. This can be a mix of explosives with a highly radioactive substance such as spent nuclear fuel, cesium used in medicine or industry, or plutonium from a nuclear weapon or conventional nuclear power station that is unsuitable for weapons manufacture.
>
> The explosion of such a bomb creates a radioactive cloud that can cause severe and very long-lasting contamination. If such a thing happened in New York, humans might have to abandon parts of the city for hundreds, if not thousands, of years.[74]

### Urban Violence and Anomie

Our world seems decidedly more and more dangerous and terrifying. But these apocalyptic scenarios, which reality is fast catching up with if not surpassing, are only the most visible, most spectacular aspects of the rising tide of violence in the last few decades. The various forms of terrorism, governmental and nongovernmental, are part of a generalized increase in urban violence. The acting executive director of the UN Center for Human Settlements (Habitat) stressed in 1998 'the growing concern about escalating urban violence'. As he described it, 'Worldwide, urban violence is estimated to have grown by approximately 4 percent a year over the last two decades. This is true not only in regions that are highly urbanized such as Europe and North America, but also in Africa, which is both the least urbanized continent and one with the highest urban growth rates.'[75]

No region of the world has been spared. In fact, by contrast with what is generally supposed, violence against persons is actually significantly more common in the West than in Asia. (Are there lessons to be drawn here about levels of 'Civilization'?) According to UN agency figures, the percentage of people who had experienced violence in urban areas with more than 100,000 inhabitants during the years 1988–94 was 11 percent in Asia and the same in Eastern Europe (before the crisis hit these two regions in 1997–8), as opposed to 15 percent in Western Europe and 20 percent in North America. Only South America (at 31 percent) and Africa (33 percent) surpassed the North American level of violence.[76]

The extent of urban violence in the United States, leader of the 'civilized world', is well known. But the statistics are still dumbfounding and give a disquieting foretaste of the future. According to one study carried out in Boston, one out of ten children between the ages of one and five has witnessed a shooting or stabbing, and about a quarter of low-income, urban youth has witnessed a murder.[77] Admittedly the 1990s saw a fall in violent crime rates in the United States, as in other Western countries, thanks to improving economic conditions. But this took place also – and sometimes above all – at the cost of a considerable increase in repression.

US Bureau of Justice Statistics figures give a clear picture. The homicide rate more than doubled from the mid-1960s, reaching 10.2 per 100,000 inhabitants with the recession in 1980. It then fell in relative terms, only to go back up to 9.8 in 1991. The sharply lower figure for 1999 (5.7) was the result of the longest economic expansion in US history, but also of an even higher growth rate: the increase in the prison population. The latter increased by an average of 6 percent a year in the 1990s, rising from 292 prisoners per 100,000 inhabitants on 31 December 1990, to 478 on 31 December 2000 – meaning a total of 1,381,892 people in jail.[78]

The universal phenomenon of rising urban violence during the last two decades is not hard to explain. Franz Vanderschueren, technical adviser to Habitat's Urban Management Program, has identified its causes quite well:

> Violence is not a spontaneous phenomenon but the product of a society characterized by inequality and exclusion and lack of institutional or social control. However, urban marginality and poverty do not automatically lead to violence, but may favour it in certain circumstances. The utter poverty of badly serviced neighbourhoods encourages violence. The Montreal Conference of Mayors (1989) identified 'the basic causes of violence increase: urban growth with marginalization of the underprivileged and the isolation of groups at risk, qualitative and quantitative insufficiency of social housing programmes and community amenities, unemployment of young people.' In a society that promotes consumption and competition to the detriment of sharing and solidarity, young people with no hope of employment or success look for ways to survive and to gain a sense of recognition at least from their peer group. This often leads to violence and youth gangs.[79]

Habitat's 2001 report on 'the state of the world's cities' helps dot the i's and cross the t's about the causes of these phenomena:

> In the 1970s, the world embarked on a phase of globalization aimed at deregulating labour markets, privatizing government functions and liberalizing finance. Financial liberalization was supposed to move savings from developed to developing countries, lower the costs of borrowing, reduce risk through new financial instruments, and increase economic growth.

Much the opposite materialized: savings have flowed from poor to richer countries, interest rates have generally increased, risk has risen and economic growth throughout the world has slowed for the vast majority of countries, rich and poor.[80]

We need to supplement this observation by noting the steadily deepening inequality among and within countries over the past two decades. This gives us a fairly complete list of the main socio-economic factors resulting in the great degree of anomie, the disintegration of social norms and reference points, characteristic of our times. Emile Durkheim, the pioneering sociologist whose study of suicide won him lasting fame, forged the concept of anomie; it served him as one major explanation among others for suicide as a social phenomenon. Durkheim thought that anomie could also explain homicides:

> Anomy, in fact, begets a state of exasperation and irritated weariness which may turn against the person himself or another according to circumstances; in the first case, we have suicide, in the second, homicide. The causes determining the direction of such overexcited forces probably depend on the agent's moral constitution.[81]

However obsolete the remedies may be that Durkheim proposed for this social problem, the essentials of his diagnosis nonetheless still seem remarkably insightful.[82] Durkheim used the term anomie as a synonym for 'deregulation', and therefore for economic deregulation as well. At the end of the nineteenth century he summed up one hundred years of capitalist development as follows: 'For a whole century, economic progress has mainly consisted in freeing industrial relations from all regulation ... Actually ... government, instead of regulating economic life, has become its tool and servant.'[83]

This has been the case once again, more massively than ever, in the last quarter century. After thirty years of almost universal, Keynesian-inspired regulation of market economies in the post-1945 period, the neoliberal offensive waged by Thatcher and Reagan (following Pinochet) triumphed on a global scale and broke through every form of resistance. Deregulation, trade liberalization and privatization have been the magic words of this neoliberal globalization. It has resulted in a tremendous anomie, never before seen on such a scale. Besides the rise of urban violence, this context has greatly fostered the rise of terrorism, international organized crime and various illicit traffics. These make up 'the dark side of globalization', as a Clinton Administration official so rightly observed.[84]

Durkheim recognized in his own time that progress could be accompanied by pathologies. He saw, to take up the terms of the discussion already begun in this chapter, that the very forward march of Civilization can be accompanied by forms of Barbarism, which can win the upper hand whenever society drifts toward anomie. He understood that this problem could only be solved through structural social change – even if the changes he advocated himself have been consigned to the dustbin of history:

> Thus, we may believe that this aggravation [of suicides] springs not from the intrinsic nature of progress but from the special conditions under which it occurs in our day, and nothing assures us that these conditions are normal. For we must not be dazzled by the brilliant development of sciences, the arts and industry of which we are the witness; this development is altogether certainly taking place in the midst of a morbid effervescence, the grievous repercussions of which every one of us feels. It is thus very possible and even probable that the rising tide of suicide originates in a pathological state just now accompanying the march of civilization without being its necessary condition ... [T]he change in moral temperament thus betrayed bears witness to a profound change in our social structure. To cure one, therefore, the other must be reformed.[85]

On top of the socio-economic factors resulting from neoliberal globalization, a political factor of great historical importance has further exacerbated the anomie of our times: the collapse of 'really existing socialism', together with the thorough discrediting of the very idea of socialism that this collapse has entailed (however wrong it may have been to identify the socialist project with 'really existing' socialism). The utopian hope for a society founded on social justice and equality, seen as an alternative to capitalism, structured the way people viewed the world politically for almost a century, and even longer in Europe. The foundering of this sense of an alternative has resulted in an extraordinary loss of ideological reference points. This has made the general anomie that much worse.

The combination of these two dimensions – socio-economic anomie together with political and ideological anomie – has inevitably led people to fall back on other factors of social solidarity such as religion, family and fatherland, as Durkheim pointed out in his own time. People's urges to reaffirm their 'identities' have been tearing our planet apart once again for several years now. The resurgence of religious fundamentalism, as we have tried to show here, is only one of their many manifestations. In order to reverse this baleful tendency, we need of course to deal with the fundamental causes built into existing social structures, as Durkheim foresaw in *Suicide*. But since we cannot transform society right away – and logically enough, so that we will be able to transform society eventually – it is necessary for a credible progressive alternative to neoliberal capitalism to emerge again. Only this kind of alternative can pull the rug out from under reactionary identity politics, by channelling social discontent toward transformative action in the pursuit of democracy and justice. This is the same approach that the last chapter took toward Islamic fundamentalism.

Slanderers today amalgamate the progressive movement struggling against neoliberal globalization with religious fundamentalism and other forms of identity-based fanaticism. Their charges are the opposite of the truth. In reality, the struggle against neoliberal globalization – born in the last years of the dying twentieth century, and growing rapidly among the new generation on this verge of the twenty-first century – is our best hope for defeating the wave of reaction.

# FOUR

# The Barbarism of the 'Civilizing Mission' [Postscript]

*Take up the White Man's burden –*
*And reap his old reward:*
*The blame of those ye better,*
*The hate of those ye guard –*
*The cry of hosts ye humour*
*(Ah, slowly!) toward the light: –*
*'Why brought ye us from bondage,*
*Our loved Egyptian night?'*

Rudyard Kipling (1899)[1]

*The shame of the 'White Man's Burden' business is ... that we attempt to deceive ourselves and each other by miscalling a campaign purely for commercial spoil a benevolent enterprise in the cause of freedom and true civilization. Its only real result is to brand us in the eyes of the keen-sighted world as the hypocrites we are.*

Chicago Commons (1899)[2]

*Colonial policy is the most recent form of barbarism, or, if you prefer, the term of civilisation.*

Anatole France (1905)[3]

In April 2003, in the wake of the fall of Baghdad, I made the following prognosis:

> As it extends its presence in the Arab world further and further, the US is stretching its troops too thin. The hatred that it evokes in all Middle Eastern countries and throughout the Islamic world has already blown up in its face several times; 11 September 2001 was only the most spectacular, deadliest manifestation so far of this hatred. The occupation of Iraq will push the general resentment to extremes; it will speed up the decomposition of the regional order backed by Washington. There will be no Pax Americana. Rather there will be another step downwards towards barbarism, with the chief barbarism of Washington and its allies sustaining the opposite barbarism of religious fanaticism.[4]

Drafting this new chapter in October 2005, I have a sad surfeit of confirmations to choose among for this prediction, which was inspired by the theses put forward in the earlier chapters. In fact illustrations of the clash of barbarisms have been so numerous in the four years since 11 September 2001 that a whole volume would not be enough to describe them, still less a single chapter. Here we must therefore be satisfied with expressing or passing along a few reflections on the tragic course of events, restricting ourselves to the part of the world that the consequences of 11 September 2001 have most seriously affected.

### Varieties of Perverse Enjoyment

The spectacle of Barbarism, or more strictly speaking the spectacle of the twin barbarisms, has tragically become an everyday occurrence in Iraq. On the one hand we have the lesser barbarism, atrocious as it nonetheless is, of Islamic fundamentalist fanatics of Wahabbite inspiration or quasi-fascist 'Saddamist' Ba'athist fanatics, above all when they stage their beheadings on film or when some of them go so far as to blow themselves up – or send people within their power to blow themselves up – so as to kill as many Iraqis as possible. Often the only thing these Iraqis have done wrong in their assassins' eyes is to be Shiites, or sometimes to have stood in line in order to get a job as a police officer or soldier, driven by the unemployment and poverty that the occupation has exacerbated, just as still others in other lands stand in line in front of the recruiting offices for underground mine workers or other high-risk jobs.

Abu Musab al-Zarqawi, whom bin Laden dubbed al-Qa'ida's Iraqi leader in October 2004, has become even more than his overlord the personification of the most criminal fanaticism.[5] He is the equivalent of the worst serial killers and mass killers dreamed up for horror movies, to the point that some people go so far as to claim that he himself is a fictional character. In any event the atrocities that he has claimed responsibility for are unfortunately not fictional, just as the suicide bombers killing Shiites are, sadly, not fictional.

Here the abomination of fanaticism has reached its apogee. If there were still some degree of distorted, vengeful morality in self-destruction aimed at inflicting major harm on an oppressive and more powerful adversary, even when the harm is indiscriminate, what justification can be invoked when people commit suicide in order to kill as many civilians as possible belonging to a community that is in a minority in the Muslim world, historically oppressed everywhere outside Iran, where it is in the majority? The bombers and their commanders have never experienced the least oppression at the hands of the Shiite community; in point of fact, the bomber responsible for one of the most murderous attacks in the series was not even Iraqi, but rather Jordanian, like Zarqawi himself. All the evidence shows that the one thing that has provoked their rage is seeing the Shiite community freed at last from the oppression that it had undergone.

The 'ecstasy' felt by André Malraux's Chen, mentioned in the previous chapter, could be seen as doubly legitimate: on the one hand, he wanted to revenge the liquidation of thousands of his comrades; on the other hand, he attempted to do so by trying to assassinate the tyrant who was chiefly responsible for the massacre. The Iraqi equivalent would have been a suicide attack aimed at assassinating Saddam Hussein when he was still in power, carried out by one of the numerous categories of his victims. But what 'ecstasy' can the people experience who blow themselves up in Iraq in order to kill indiscriminately the erstwhile victims, while the Shiites have avoided either taking massive, bloody revenge after the tyranny's fall or acting in concert with the invading troops, as the warlords of the Northern Alliance did in Afghanistan?

The summit of murderous fanaticism has been reached in Iraq since the forces led by Washington occupied the country. Mass murders have become so common in this martyred country, whose tribulations have been intensifying continuously since the Ba'athist seizure of power in 1968, that they are seen as commonplace and treated as minor 'other news' by the international media – except when, from time to time, the number of victims of an attack approaches or exceeds a hundred, like the tolling of a macabre clock punctuating the tick-tock of its pendulum.

This barbarism, a lesser one in a quantitative sense, is inexorably fuelled by the ordeal and spectacle of the other, greater barbarism. When the earlier chapters of this book were being written, the greater barbarism orchestrated from Washington still had only one topographical name with symbolic renonance to add to its post-11 September honours list: Guantánamo. Since then two other symbolic names have been added: Fallujah and, above all, Abu Ghraib. 'Above all' in this case refers only to the relative originality of what was revealed, and is clearly not based on the number of victims.

As with the invasion of Iraq in 1991, estimates vary widely of the number of deaths caused by the 2003 invasion. They range from ten thousand or more, as official and semi-official US and British sources are willing to admit, to one hundred thousand or more, according to the study published in October 2004 by the British medical journal *The Lancet*.[6] Even the lower figure, admitted by the occupiers, would be an enormous price to inflict on a people, even in the interest of freeing them from a tyrant.[7]

The destruction of the city of Fallujah was one more illustration of the brutality that US military forces are capable of in the course of their imperial expeditions. This brutality is considerably, and paradoxically, aggravated by the 'surgical' precision of their strikes, when they no longer aim at limiting immediate 'collateral damage' but rather focus their firepower directly on an urban conglomeration inhabited by civilians. Fallujah was, on the scale of a city of almost 300,000 inhabitants, the equivalent of the US AC-130 bombing on 1 July 2002 of a wedding in Afghanistan, with 'high-precision munitions' that caused about fifty deaths and about a hundred casualties in the crowd. The difference was that what happened in Afghanistan was a 'blunder', while those who ordered the deadly assaults on Fallujah were fully aware of what they were doing.

From one offensive to the next in the Sunni Arab area of Iraq, the US armed forces are crushing the civilian population under their bulldozer, while many of the forces they are fighting against simply move around to other spots in the same area. Senator John McCain made this observation when he questioned General George W. Casey, commander of the 'multinational force' in Iraq, during a hearing before the Armed Services Committee of the US Senate in September 2005: 'How many times, General Casey, are we going to read about another offensive in Fallujah, Mosul, Ramadi, al-Qaim, where we go in, we take control, and we leave, and the bad guys come back again?'[8]

In reality the very brutality of the assaults, if not the mere presence of occupation troops, on balance adds more to the stream of new volunteers joining the 'insurgents' than it eliminates combatants among them. General Casey recognized this himself when he said during the same hearings that the presence of 'the coalition forces as an occupying force' was 'one of the elements that [fuel] the insurgency'. There is nothing much new in this respect. The observation is as old as the era of decolonization, which made the colonial policies of the nineteenth and early twentieth centuries – the 'most recent form of barbarism', as Anatole France called them – intolerable. Since then, peoples of occupied countries refuse to lay down their arms before ridding themselves of their occupiers.

Abu Ghraib, by contrast, had the impact of an electric shock on a major part of US public opinion. Showing methods that people had thought were limited to armies of inherently barbarous regimes, it was one of the most powerful revelations of the regression of the contemporary United States towards Barbarism. Since the scandal of the sequences of torture photographed and filmed in Iraq's Abu Ghraib military prison burst onto the front pages in April 2004, other examples of barbaric behaviour by members of the US armed forces have come to light. They confirm that the moral degeneration that the scandal bore witness to is not some isolated phenomenon that has been done away with since it was 'discovered'.

Moreover, the photos that have been made public and been viewed around the world are only part of the photography done at Abu Ghraib. The Pentagon has others, just as shocking and repulsive, if not more so, and refuses to release them out of fear of blemishing its reputation still further.[9] But these images in any case only give a mitigated taste of a horror of which they only captured a few fleeting moments. In order to gauge the extent of the perversion of the tortures carried out, it is necessary to read the statements gathered from the victims as part of the military authorities' investigation at the beginning of the scandal, before it burst onto the television screens. They bear the strongest possible witness to barbarism at work. The *Washington Post* has published some transcripts of them on its Internet site.[10]

Before as well as after the fact, many investigations by US journalists have shown that the tortures at Abu Ghraib were part of a systematic logic, which rejects international conventions and dehumanizes the detainees. In the list of new words for *Untermenschen*, just under the 'unlawful combatants' at Guantánamo, we must add the official term used by the US armed forces to designate their detainees in Afghanistan as well as in Iraq: 'Persons Under Control' or PUCs – pronounced 'pucks' (to be struck like ice hockey pucks!). The Bush Administration, one of the most sinister in US history, put the logic of negating human rights and the 'chain of command' that regulate the ill-treatment in place in the weeks after 11 September 2001.[11] Only the disclosure of the torture through leaks of photos and videos to the media was not on the original programme.

The report published in September 2005 by the US organization Human Rights Watch on the torture of Iraqi detainees at Forward Operation Base Mercury, to the east of Fallujah, comes to the same conclusions. This document has made fresh revelations to add to the occupation forces' catalogue of barbarities:[12]

The abuses alleged in this report can be traced to the Bush Administration's decision to disregard the Geneva Conventions in the armed conflict in Afghanistan.

On February 7, 2002, President George W. Bush announced that the Geneva Conventions concerning the treatment of prisoners did not apply at all to al-Qa'ida members or to Taliban soldiers because they did not qualify as members of the armed forces. He insisted that detainees would nonetheless be treated 'humanely.' Defense Secretary Donald Rumsfeld told journalists that day: 'The reality is the set of facts that exist today with al-Qa'ida and the Taliban were not necessarily the set of facts that were considered when the Geneva Conventions [sic] was fashioned.'

The accounts presented in this report are further evidence that this decision by the Bush Administration was to have a profound influence on the treatment of detained persons in military operations in Iraq as well as in the 'global war on terror.' In short, the refusal to apply the Geneva Conventions to Guantánamo Bay and Afghanistan was to undermine long-standing adherence by the US armed forces to federal law and the laws of armed conflict concerning the proper treatment of prisoners.[13]

... [T]here is increasing evidence that high-ranking US civilian and military leaders made decisions and issued policies that facilitated serious and widespread violations of the law. The circumstances strongly suggest that they either knew or should have known that such violations took place as a result of their actions. There is also mounting information that, when presented with evidence that abuse was in fact occurring, they failed to act to stop it.[14]

The Bush Administration's responsibility for the horrors committed by the US armed forces in Afghanistan and Iraq is however a settled case; only the administration's unconditional supporters can still blame the horrors on a few 'bad apples'. The problem is nonetheless much more serious. The acts of barbarism committed in the two countries invaded after 11 September 2001 reveal a more general regression affecting a substantial part of US society, of which the Bush Administration itself is the most obvious manifestation.

This is the regression that US writer Susan Sontag emphasized in her admirable reflections on the roots of the barbarism revealed in Iraq. No one has commented more insightfully on the Abu Ghraib tortures than she did in one of her last articles, published in May 2004, seven months before her death. It deserves to be cited at length:

> What makes some actions representative and others not? The issue is not whether the torture was done by individuals (i.e., 'not by everybody') – but whether it was systematic. Authorized. Condoned. All acts are done by individuals. The issue is not whether a majority or a minority of Americans performs such acts but whether the nature of the policies prosecuted by this administration and the hierarchies deployed to carry them out makes such acts likely.
>
> Considered in this light, the photographs are us. That is, they are representative of the fundamental corruptions of any foreign occupation together with the Bush Administration's distinctive policies ...
>
> ... [T]he horror of what is shown in the photographs cannot be separated from the horror that the photographs were taken – with the perpetrators posing, gloating, over their helpless captives. German soldiers in the Second World War took photographs of the atrocities they were committing in Poland and Russia, but snapshots in which the executioners placed themselves among their victims are exceedingly rare ... If there is something comparable to what these pictures show it would be some of the photographs of black victims of lynching taken between the 1880's and 1930's, which show Americans grinning beneath the naked mutilated body of a black man or woman hanging behind them from a tree ...
>
> Looking at these photographs, you ask yourself, How can

someone grin at the sufferings and humiliation of another human being? Set guard dogs at the genitals and legs of cowering naked prisoners? Force shackled, hooded prisoners to masturbate or simulate oral sex with one another? And you feel naive for asking, since the answer is, self-evidently, People do these things to other people. Rape and pain inflicted on the genitals are among the most common forms of torture. Not just in Nazi concentration camps and in Abu Ghraib when it was run by Saddam Hussein. Americans, too, have done and do them when they are told, or made to feel, that those over whom they have absolute power deserve to be humiliated, tormented. They do them when they are led to believe that the people they are torturing belong to an inferior race or religion. For the meaning of these pictures is not just that these acts were performed, but that their perpetrators apparently had no sense that there was anything wrong in what the pictures show.

Even more appalling, since the pictures were meant to be circulated and seen by many people: it was all fun. And this idea of fun is, alas, more and more – contrary to what President Bush is telling the world – part of 'the true nature and heart of America.' It is hard to measure the increasing acceptance of brutality in American life, but its evidence is everywhere ... America has become a country in which the fantasies and the practice of violence are seen as good entertainment, fun.[15]

After the Abu Ghraib scandal came out into the open, the newspaper headlines in Iraq, the Arab world and the Islamic world as a whole commented almost in unison, 'Their freedom and their democracy equal torture and pornography.' It was a year after the fall of Baghdad, accompanied by a sack of the city and of the country's cultural heritage under the benevolent gaze of the US occupation troops – a sack unparalleled since the one that Hulagu Khan's Mongol hordes carried out in 1258. Unlike George W. Bush's troops, Hulagu's hordes had had no pretension of incarnating Civilization with a capital C; they belonged in fact to a much cruder society than the one whose territory they were invading. The inhabitants of the Abbasid caliphate, under which Arab-Islamic civilization had experienced its Eastern golden age before beginning the decline from which it has still not recovered, considered the Mongols barbarians.

George W. Bush's hordes for their part – or at least their political and military leaders – are decked out in all the material finery of modern Western civilization, despite their lack of inspiration from its moral and spiritual heritage. The 'Green Zone' within which the occupation authorities – previously the 'Coalition Provisional Authority' (CPA) – have shut themselves up was created in the image of the 'gated communities' mentioned in the last chapter. We need only read the description given by the *Washington Post*'s special correspondent to appreciate this:

> Life inside the high-security Green Zone – what some CPA staffers jokingly call the Emerald City – bears little resemblance to that in the rest of Baghdad. The power is always on. Shiny shuttle buses zip passengers around. Outdoor cafes stay open late into the night.
>
> There is little effort to comply with Islamic traditions. Beer flows freely at restaurants. Women walk around in shorts. Bacon cheeseburgers are on the CPA's lunch menu.
>
> 'It's like a different planet,' said an Iraqi American who has a senior position in the CPA and lives in the Green Zone but regularly ventures out to see relatives. 'It's cut off from the real Iraq.'[16]

In an extraordinary paradox, after the new sack of Baghdad the troops of a country that prides itself on representing Civilization, and on transmitting it to Muslims who are viewed with contempt as a sort of barbarians, have themselves come to be viewed by the inhabitants of the conquered country, and by the Muslim world as a whole, as the embodiment of a modern, perverse form of Barbarism. The era of the 'new imperialism', which its advocates imagined would be as 'glorious' as the era of nineteenth-century imperialism, has begun so badly that we may be justified in hoping that it will be much shorter.

*The 'Civilizing Mission's' New Clothes*

Even more than George W. Bush and his speechwriters, Britain's Labour Prime Minister Tony Blair has expressed in the crudest fashion the neo-imperialist doctrine that has become the official discourse of his zealous alliance with the most reactionary administration in US history or in the contemporary West. This came in a speech Blair gave on 2 October 2001, three weeks after the 11 September attacks, in front of his party's annual conference at Brighton, a speech that – 'unusually', according to *The Guardian*[17] – he had written himself:

> So I believe this is a fight for freedom. And I want to make it a fight for justice too. Justice not only to punish the guilty. But justice to bring those same values of democracy and freedom to people round the world ...
>
> The starving, the wretched, the dispossessed, the ignorant, those living in want and squalor from the deserts of Northern Africa to the slums of Gaza, to the mountain ranges of Afghanistan: they too are our cause.
>
> This is a moment to seize. The Kaleidoscope has been shaken. The pieces are in flux. Soon they will settle again. Before they do, let us re-order this world around us.[18]

'A messianic speech' was the admiring comment of Niall Ferguson, the chief British academic devotee of the 'new imperialism', as he calls it himself,[19] adding right away that apart from grandiloquent speeches the United States is the only country capable of playing this role in today's world. The historian commented that 'it is hard to think of a Prime Minister since Gladstone so ready to make what sounds remarkably like undiluted altruism the basis of his foreign policy ... On reflection, this bears more than a passing resemblance to the Victorians' project to export their own "civilization" to the world.'[20]

*The Guardian* had already noted the resemblance between Blair's and Gladstone's speeches.[21] But as it happens it was a minister, Joseph Chamberlain, who gave the speech most analogous to Blair's and Bush's. Chamberlain resigned from Gladstone's cabinet in 1886 as a sign of his even more imperialist sentiments. He was in fact the main ideologue of 'imperialism' in the industrial era at the end of the nineteenth century, particularly when he served as Colonial Secretary between 1895 and 1903. In a celebrated speech on the new conception of empire, delivered in 1897, he declared:

> [W]e have now reached the third stage in our history, and the true conception of our Empire.
>
> ... [T]he sense of possession has given place to a different sentiment – the sense of obligation. We feel now that our rule over these territories can only be justified if we can show that it adds to the happiness and prosperity of the people, and I maintain that our rule does, and has, brought security and peace and comparative prosperity to countries that never knew these blessings before.
>
> In carrying out this work of civilization we are fulfilling what I believe to be our national mission, and we are finding scope for the exercise of these faculties and qualities which have made of us a great governing race ... No doubt, in the first instance, when these conquests have been made, there has been bloodshed, there has been loss of life among the native populations, loss of still more precious lives among those who have been sent out to bring these countries into some kind of disciplined order, but it must be remembered that that is the condition of the mission we have to fulfil ...
>
> You cannot have omelettes without breaking eggs; you cannot destroy the practices of barbarism, of slavery, of superstition, which for centuries have desolated the interior of Africa, without the use of force; but if you will fairly contrast the gain to humanity with the price which we are bound to pay for it, I think you may well rejoice in the result of such expeditions as those which have been recently conducted ...[22]

More than a century later the same arguments, virtually the same words (allowing for a bit of latter-day self-censorship), can be heard from the mouths of the champions of the new imperial expeditions. The passage of time seems to have erased to some extent the discredit or even opprobrium that pretensions of this kind encountered in the period after decolonization. One might have thought in fact that imperialist rhetoric of this specifically late nineteenth-century type had died out for good. This was the rhetoric that led King Leopold II of the Belgians to say in 1876, before about ten million Congolese died a few years later on the altar of his private interests, in one of the most horrific episodes in the history of colonial barbarity – in the heart of darkness:[23]

> To open up to civilization the only part of the planet where it has still not yet penetrated; to piece the shadows that shroud entire peoples: this, if I may dare to say it, is a crusade worthy of this century of progress. It is a question of raising the banner of civilization on Central Africa's soil and of struggling against the slave trade.[24]

And yet we see this same rhetoric resurfacing on the occasion of the new imperial wars waged by the Bush-Blair duo, in a way that advocates of the manifest destiny of the 'Anglo-Saxon race' during the nineteenth century would certainly have appreciated very much.[25] Admittedly the times have changed to the point that it could no longer be the main argument – not to say the main pretext – used to justify invading Iraq. In the absence of genocide in progress,[26] US and British public opinion would not have accepted their countries' armies involving themselves in a major war solely in order to overthrow a tyrant and establish a democratic regime.

We may also note that even in the nineteenth century the argument about the 'civilizing mission' was never the one that really motivated rulers or convinced their peoples. It only served as a hypocritical tool to soothe their consciences as they undertook colonial expeditions that were in reality dictated by economic interests, as the Chicago Commons editorial cited as an epigraph for this chapter mentioned at the end of the century. But this argument no longer serves to mobilize people either. The development of consciousness and the advance of

Civilization have led to people's not even being inclined any more to wage colonial wars – to see their soldiers kill and be killed – purely for the sake of economic interests.

This is why the main argument invoked since 11 September 2001 has been terrorism. The 'war against terrorism' is the generic title under which the wars in Afghanistan and Iraq were waged. The argument was plausible in the case of the Afghanistan intervention, inasmuch as the al-Qa'ida network was based there, if we discount the considerations that have already been laid out in this book.[27] It was a purely mendacious argument in the case of Iraq, as the world-wide anti-war movement pointed out continually before the war, culminating on 15 February 2003 in an international mobilization on an unprecedented scale. Very quickly after Iraq was occupied the anti-war movement proved to be right.

The pretext of terrorism and the fable of the 'weapons of mass destruction' hidden in Iraq managed to convince the majority of US public opinion – traumatized by 11 September 2001 and by the climate of fear deliberately maintained by the Bush Administration with its fanfare of 'yellow' and 'orange' alerts – of the merits of invading Iraq in order to overthrow Saddam Hussein and eliminate the phantom weapons. But they were not enough to justify Iraq's lengthy occupation, which was of course essential to the project. As innumerable commentators, including the present author,[28] explained, the goal of George W. Bush and the Project for a New American Century (PNAC) – the main group pressing for the Iraq invasion, from which several members and co-workers of the Bush Administration emerged[29] – was primarily and essentially strategic, in the broad sense of the term.

The link between the US hold over Iraq and the objective of a new 'American century' relates to the importance, both economic and military, of controlling the oil of the Arab-Persian Gulf. Gulf oil constitutes two-thirds of the global reserves of this energy source, which is forecast to dry up in the course of the twenty-first century – a fact that raises oil's strategic value and price considerably. Through its direct protectorate over the Saudi kingdom and the emirates of Kuwait and Qatar, where it has a military presence, the US already controls a third of the world's proven oil reserves. By adding Iraq, the share falling under its direct control reaches 43 percent. And here we are only considering proven reserves; these countries' share of probable reserves, and Iraq's share in particular, is even higher.[30]

Long-term control over Iraq, and nothing less, is therefore the most important of the strategic stakes. Consequently Washington needed from the beginning to supply another pretext to complement its fairytales about terrorism, in order to justify a long-term presence in the country. The argument of 'democratization' was the obvious best choice. On 26 February 2003, one month before invading Iraq, George W. Bush gave a speech laying out his programme for Iraq and the Middle East to the American Enterprise Institute, a think tank well known as a haunt of 'neo-conservatives', twenty of whom the president boasted of having 'borrowed' for his administration. After devoting the first point of his speech to the 'war against terrorism' and weapons of mass destruction, as was required, Bush added these very revealing remarks:

> Rebuilding Iraq will require a sustained commitment from many nations, including our own: we will remain in Iraq as long as necessary, and not a day more. America has made and kept this kind of commitment before – in the peace that followed a world war. After defeating enemies, we did not leave behind occupying armies, we left constitutions and parliaments. We established an atmosphere of safety, in which responsible, reform-minded local leaders could build lasting institutions of freedom. In societies that once bred fascism and militarism, liberty found a permanent home.
>
> There was a time when many said that the cultures of Japan and Germany were incapable of sustaining democratic values. Well, they were wrong. Some say the same of Iraq today. They are mistaken. [31]

In short, Bush promised that the US would only remain in Iraq as long as necessary, as it did after 1945 in Germany and Japan – two countries where the US still maintains military bases sixty years later!

The example of the two major countries defeated in the Second World War was invoked constantly during the months when the invasion of Iraq was being prepared and the initial phase of the occupation. The Rand Corporation, one of the Pentagon's principal think tanks, which Donald Rumsfeld had presided over during the Reagan years and on the board of which Condoleezza Rice sat during the following decade, even produced a book devoted to the lessons of past US experiences in the field of 'nation-building', with the German and Japanese cases as starting points.[32]

Noah Feldman, professor of law at New York University, enlisted as a 'constitutional adviser' by the Iraq occupation authorities, has told an anecdote that is significant in this respect. In May 2003, in the airplane that was taking him to Iraq along with several dozen other advisers specialized in various fields,

> I glanced around at my new colleagues. Those who were awake were reading intently. When I saw what they were reading, though, a chill crept over me ... Not one seemed to need a refresher on Iraq or the Gulf region. Without exception, they were reading new books on the American occupation and reconstruction of Germany and Japan.[33]

The United States thus undertook its work in Iraq inspired by the firm conviction that it was making a remake of 1945. Leaving aside the grotesque nature of this illusion, we can note one major difference that no one, however impassioned, could miss: in 1945, the US under Roosevelt contributed decisively to drafting the UN Charter, which has become the cornerstone of international public law. In 2003 the same US, together with the UK, violated international law and the UN Charter in the most brazen way possible.

From this angle alone the invasion of Iraq made a major contribution to replacing the rule of law with the 'law of the jungle' in international relations, exactly contrary to what George Bush Senior had promised in 1990. Solely from this point of view the invasion of Iraq, the apogee of the hegemonic unilateralism analysed in the previous chapter, represents a decisive step in the regression of the society of nations from Civilization to Barbarism. This aspect of the problem has been commented on widely. Let us return instead to examining the 'civilizing mission' that the Bush administration has taken upon itself in Iraq and the Middle East.

## The 'Democracy Paradox'

I am often glad, as in chapter 2 of this book, to cite and comment on what Samuel Huntington called the 'democracy paradox': the fact that the kind of electoral democracy born in the West often brings leaders to power outside the West who are hostile to Western domination.[34] This 'paradox' was very much present in the Bush administration's minds when it launched its campaign in the Middle East following 11 September 2001. Until 2004 the administration's claims that its military expeditions aimed at fostering democracy could fool only the naïve or ignorant.

   In point of fact, there was a flagrant contradiction between these ideological claims – which only a few singular individuals among the 'neoconservatives' gathered around the Pentagon actually seemed to believe, with the faith of simpletons – and the Bush administration's real practices, like those of earlier administrations. One of the best-known US experts in the field of 'democracy promotion' described this very classically Machiavellian contradiction, not long before the invasion of Iraq, as a 'split presidential personality' syndrome. He recalled the most recent outbreaks of this disease, whose bacilli seem to have taken up permanent residence in the White House.

> President Clinton made liberal use of pro-democracy rhetoric and did support democracy in many places, but throughout his presidency, US security and economic interests – whether in China, Egypt, Jordan, Kazakhstan, Saudi Arabia, Vietnam, or various other countries – frequently trumped an interest in democracy. The same was true in the George H. W. Bush Administration and certainly also under Ronald Reagan, whose outspoken support for freedom in the communist

world was accompanied by close US relations with various authoritarian regimes useful to the United States, such as those led by Suharto in Indonesia, Mobutu Sese Seko in Zaïre, the generals of Nigeria, and the Institutional Revolutionary Party of Mexico.

George W. Bush is thus scarcely the first US president to evidence a split personality on democracy promotion.[35]

The expert on democratization had no difficulty in illustrating his remarks with examples from the Bush II Administration, referring to facts some of which this book has already mentioned: in his own words, the 'bear hug' for putsch leader General Pervez Musharraf; the friendship with 'the autocratic leaders of Uzbekistan, Kazakhstan, and Kyrgyzstan,' as well as with 'the totalitarian megalomaniac running Turkmenistan'; inversely, the eagerness to 'accept' the April 2002 coup attempt against Venezuela's Hugo Chavez; and the statements warning that the popular re-election of Palestinian President Yasir Arafat would be 'unacceptable'.

The list of countries cited above is certainly not exhaustive. One country in particular is conspicuous by its absence: Azerbaijan, another oil-rich Muslim state governed by a despotic ruler, Ilham Aliyev, whose father ran the country for almost thirty years before handing power over to him. An editorial in the *Washington Post* has put the facts about Aliyev plainly:

> Pentagon officials argue that Azerbaijan is vital to the war on terrorism ... But a more obvious source of President Bush's policy is oil. Over the last decade, Mr Aliyev and his father granted billions in contracts to such companies as BP-Amoco, ChevronTexaco and ExxonMobil. He also has supported a $3 billion pipeline that is to carry oil from the Caspian to a port in Turkey. According to Mr Aliyev, Mr Bush once pronounced him an honorary citizen of Texas in appreciation of his support for American oil companies.[36]

So there was nothing really new in the duplicity shown by the Bush Administration after 11 September 2001. A major turning point occurred, however, in the Iraq affair in autumn 2003. Beginning in September, leaks emanating from the Iraq Survey Group (ISG), which the previous June the occupying coalition had put in charge of finding the 'weapons of mass destruction' that had been the chief official pretext for invading Iraq, were already indicating that there weren't any.[37] The ISG's interim report in October confirmed this information. The resignation and admissions by David Kay, former chief inspector for the United Nations Special Commission (Unscom) and subsequently head of the inspection force set up by the occupation authorities (who in addition was working for the CIA the whole time) followed in January 2004.

Faced in a most embarrassing way with the steady exposure of the threadbare story of 'weapons of mass destruction' that his team had intoned in order to justify its old plan of invading Iraq, George W. Bush considered it necessary to crank up the volume on his democratic argumentation. To this end, on 6 November 2003 at the US Chamber of Commerce, he gave a speech with programmatic aspirations to the National Endowment for Democracy, a bipartisan think tank and large-scale international funding agency set up in 1983 at the initiative of the Reagan administration. Making democracy in the Islamic world the central theme of his speech, the US president singled out for praise leaders of a long list of autocratic Arab countries – Morocco, Bahrain, Oman, Qatar, Yemen, Kuwait, Jordan, and even the Saudi monarchy – for the democratic progress they had made, while castigating 'the Palestinian leaders who block and undermine democratic reform'.[38] Then he devoted the last part of his speech to assuring his listeners that his administration is working to establish democracy in Iraq.

A few days later, on 15 November, the Coalition Provisional Authority (CPA) – the protectorate government run by the US in Baghdad under the leadership of Paul Bremer, whom even the London *Economist* did not hesitate to call 'the proconsul' – announced an agreement with the Iraqi Governing Council (IGC) that it had itself appointed. The agreement provided that the IGC would adopt an interim constitution drafted under the CPA's aegis at the end of February 2004. This would prepare the way for the formation of a transitional national assembly, which on 30 June would elect a provisional government that would assume 'full sovereign powers' and lead to the dissolution of the CPA.

Under this plan 'caucuses' would be organized in each of Iraq's eighteen provinces in order to choose the members of the transitional assembly that would in turn designate the provisional government. Participation in these caucuses would have to be approved by eleven out of fifteen members of an organizing committee selected by the CPA-appointed IGC and by local and provincial councils appointed directly by the CPA.

Barely two weeks after it was announced, a democratic challenge put this project of the occupation authorities, based wholly on selection and appointment, in jeopardy. The challenge came from a source as paradoxical in this role as Ayatollah Khomeini was when he led the opposition to the Shah of Iran in the name of democracy. To the great displeasure of Paul Bremer and his Iraqi associates, Grand Ayatollah Ali al-Husseini al-Sistani – the chief spiritual authority of Iraq's Shiites, who make up a majority of its population – announced his rejection of the plan. He demanded direct, immediate election by the Iraqi people as a whole of representatives to a transitional constituent assembly.

Iraq's most prominent Shiite theologian had already got in the way of Bremer's designs as early as June 2003 by rejecting the project that 'the proconsul' had initially put forward to have a definitive constitution approved by referendum before any direct elections were organized. In short, Bremer sought to 'put a lock' on Iraq's political future – as he did for its economy through the ruinous ultra-liberal reforms that he imposed – and ensure the necessary conditions to enable the US to perpetuate its domination of Iraq indefinitely, before allowing any elections on the basis of universal suffrage. Inversely, the Ayatollah was eager to allow Iraq's Shiite community to exercise the decisive influence on government that it is entitled to aspire to under a democratic regime thanks to its popular majority.

On 21 June a 'Group of Believers' posed the following question to the Ayatollah:

In the Name of Allah, the Merciful, the Compassionate
Your Eminence our Dear Marja' Grand Ayatullah Sayyid
Ali al-Husseini al-Sistani (long may he live).

*Assalamu alaikum warahmatullah wabarakatuh*
The occupying forces in Iraq have announced their decision
to establish an assembly to prepare the next Iraqi Constitution,
and that they will appoint the members of this assembly after
consulting political and social groups in the country. Then the
constitution drafted by the assembly will be presented for a
general referendum.

Kindly clarify the position toward this plan according to
the Sharia and what the believers must do regarding this matter
of drafting the Iraqi Constitution.

Sistani's response was published on 26 June:

In the Name of the Almighty
These forces have no jurisdiction whatsoever to appoint
members of the assembly drafting the constitution. There
is also no guarantee either that this assembly will prepare a
constitution that serves the best interests of the Iraqi people
and expresses its national identity, whose main pillars include
the rightful Islamic religion and noble social values. The said
plan is therefore unacceptable in essence. There must be, first of
all, a general election so that every Iraqi eligible to vote chooses
someone to represent him ['generic' masculine in original] in
a Constitutional Assembly for the drafting of the constitution.
Then the constitution drafted by this Assembly shall be put to
a referendum. All believers must demand the accomplishment
of this crucial matter and contribute to its achievement in the
best possible way. May Allah, the Blessed and Almighty, guide
everyone to that which is good and right. *Wassalamu alaikum
warahmatullah wabarakatuh.*[39]

Bremer's new plan, adopted in November 2003, was a concession to the Ayatollah. It provided that the definitive constitution would be drafted by an assembly chosen in direct elections in March 2005 before being submitted to popular vote. Sistani nonetheless judged the concession insufficient; he continued obstinately to demand that direct elections be organized in the near future, in place of the undemocratic process of selection/appointment of a transitional assembly foreseen in the CPA-IGC agreement.

In this unprecedented tussle between the representative of the world's greatest power and a 73-year-old spiritual leader living as a recluse in Najaf, it was the Shiite theologian who wielded the argument of democracy against the occupier, despite the latter's repackaging of its 'civilizing mission' as 'democratization'. The paradox – a genuine paradox this time – was heightened by the fact that Ayatollah Sistani, like Ayatollah Khomeini before him, adheres to a literal, rigorist interpretation of Islam, which in questions of daily life is as far removed from modernity as it could be. Its spirit is thoroughly retrograde, even in contrast to the spirit manifested in the work of a Muslim reformer like the Egyptian Mohammad Abduh as early as a century ago.[40]

Faced with this highly embarrassing challenge, Washington's representative and his Iraqi associates took refuge in technical arguments to claim that it was impossible to hold elections in the near future in Iraq. Their main argument was the lack of reliable voters' lists. Relying on other experts, Sistani exposed the pretext, pointing to the possibility of using the rolls for food rationing that had been used in the context of the embargo imposed on Iraq until 2003.[41] In face of the tireless insistence of some IGC members favourable to Bremer's plan, the Ayatollah proposed mediation by a commission of independent experts to be appointed by the UN.

Washington thought it could dispose of the problem, and avoid running the risk of being repudiated by the experts, by asking UN Secretary-General Kofi Annan to intervene. Annan is always glad to accommodate the US, to which he owes his job, when he can; he wrote a letter confirming the US standpoint. Sistani considered the letter offensive. He had not asked for a 'fatwa'[42] from Annan, issued from New York into the bargain; he had asked for an investigation by experts on the spot. Annan in cooperation with Washington parried by sending to Iraq a UN mission led by Lakhdar Brahimi, who had shown his mettle in the field of 'nation-building' under US control in both Haiti and Afghanistan.[43]

But in the meantime the Ayatollah had launched a resounding warning shot by having his followers, and in particular the Supreme Council of the Islamic Revolution in Iraq (SCIRI), organize impressive mass demonstrations in January with 'Yes to elections, No to appointments!' as their main slogan.

Faced with the scale of the demonstrations, the Bush Administration feared that a head-on collision would discredit for good its claims of carrying out a democratic mission in Iraq, the subsidiary pretext that had become its main one after the collapse of the 'weapons of mass destruction' fable. It was forced to give in and agree to organize elections on the basis of universal suffrage according to the procedure Sistani had advocated. However, it tried to push the date as far back as possible. On 8 March 2004 Bremer forced his draft interim constitution through by promulgating a 'Law of Administration for the State of Iraq for the Transitional Period', the so-called Transitional Administrative Law (TAL).

General elections were planned to take place at a date no later than 31 January 2005, in order to elect a provisional constituent assembly that would launch a constitutional process that was supposed to conclude by 15 October 2005. The Transitional Administrative Law – which Ayatollah Sistani opposed in vain – included an essentially undemocratic time bomb, inspired by the most classical of all recipes from the imperial cookbook that Bremer used with abandon from the moment of his arrival: *divide et impera*.[44]

From the beginning in fact Washington played the card of ethnic and religious divisions among the Iraqi people in order to perpetuate its ascendancy as an arbiter among the people's components and protector of its minorities. Washington has relied on its most faithful allies, the Kurdish leaderships, who owe their real autonomy and the relative prosperity that Iraqi Kurdistan has enjoyed since 1991 to the US protectorate. At the same time the US authorities have increasingly exploited dissensions between Shiite and Sunni Arabs as it saw more threats to its power in Iraq. Washington's appointment of Iyad Allawi, advocate of rehabilitating the members of the Ba'athist apparatus, to the post of prime minister of the provisional government that took office on 28 June 2004 was part of this approach, the aim of which was to use Sunni Arabs as a counterweight to the parties allied with Iran, who have majority support among Arab Shiites.[45]

The elections did take place on 30 January 2005, thanks to Sistani's intransigence and despite attempts by the US and their stooge Allawi to postpone them, in hopes that Allawi's chances to win a substantial share of the seats in parliament would grow over time. They chose accordingly to launch the second US assault on Fallujah in November 2004, thus creating such a situation of insecurity in the Sunni areas that the Sunnis ended up boycotting the electoral process. Sistani refused to yield to calls for postponement, which he saw as a manoeuvre. As was predictable the elections were a defeat for Washington and its stooge, and gave a parliamentary majority to the alliance dominated by the Shiite parties close to Iran, the main US enemy in the region. Nevertheless, Washington has resorted since then to all of its military and economic ascendancy over the Iraqi situation in order to keep control of the game, using to the hilt the tactic consisting of sowing discord among the various Iraqi factions.

By providing that a minimum of two-thirds of voters in at least three provinces could block adoption of the constitution drafted by the elected National Assembly in the referendum on ratification for which the deadline had been set of 15 October 2005, the TAL reinforced considerably the religious dynamic in a country where most provinces are inhabited largely by members of one or another of the Iraqi population's three main components. Naturally the apparent justification for this rule was the desire to protect the Kurdish people's right to self-determination; but in this case this was the worst possible way to guarantee this right, entirely legitimate though it is.

In effect the Transitional Administrative Law gave the Kurds – and Washington by the same token – the power of veto not only over issues of concern to them, but also over issues that in no way had anything particular or specific to do with them. By introducing this veto power through the clause about two-thirds of three provinces, the TAL also gave it to the Shiite and Sunni Arabs, encouraging the respective leaders of these communities to address themselves to their co-religionists, rather than fostering a unitary dynamic encouraging political forces to address themselves to the different components of the population, which would have been a priority for any well-intentioned lawmaker. This would have been the case, for example, if the TAL, instead of demanding a ratification by simple majority vote linked to a regional veto, had required ratification by two-thirds of the entire electorate, without any regional veto.

The rights of the Kurds could have been guaranteed in a parallel agreement among all of the country's major political forces. This would not have been at all difficult to obtain, inasmuch as the autonomy of Kurdistan – a principle that the Ba'athist regime itself had formally accepted in the accord of 11 March 1970 – is the subject of a broad consensus in post-Saddam Iraq. As for guaranteeing that these rights be respected in practice, no legislative document alone can ensure that, as everyone knows. It does not require any US guarantee for all that; Iraqi Kurdistan has a military force of its own, clearly superior to the Iraqi army now being rebuilt. Given the pace at which events are unfolding in Iraq, the Iraqi army will not be capable of constituting a threat to Kurdistan anytime soon. As for the distant future, a UN guarantee could have been granted the Kurds, which would have been in reality far more reassuring than a US protectorate.[46]

Furthermore, the conditions during the first months of the occupation were much more propitious to the unfolding of a calm democratic process than they have subsequently become. If the occupiers had announced as early as the spring of 2003 the election in the short term of a transitional constituent assembly, as Sistani demanded, in order to create a provisional government with which they would have agreed on a timetable for withdrawing their troops, Iraq would very probably be in a much better state today.

Instead Bremer left Iraq with a poisoned legacy; the situation in this ravaged country has worsened continually since the occupation began; and one must either be singularly myopic or stupidly credulous towards the sales patter of George W. Bush and other members of his administration in order to imagine that it is steadily improving. We are left with the sole hope that Iraq's tragic descent into barbarism – propelled by the irruption of a barbarous occupation into the heart of a society overwhelmed by decades of barbarous tyranny, in a regional environment that Washington's policies are continually making more barbaric – can be turned around in the short or middle term.

Having bungled its 'democratizing mission' in Iraq, has the Bush Administration succeeded, as it claims, in pulling off the miracle of establishing a modern democracy in Afghanistan? This is in any event not the conclusion that the human rights organization Afghanistan Justice Project (AJP), which brings together Afghan and international experts, has reached. In a report published in July 2005 on war crimes committed in Afghanistan from the April 1978 putsch until the US invasion, the AJP was forced to make this bitter, and entirely correct, observation:

> Although the original mandate of the Afghanistan Justice Project was to document war crimes only through 2001, some patterns of abuse identified in this report have continued in the years since 2001 ... US forces allied themselves with commanders who were responsible for some of the worst war crimes committed during the civil war. They did so because they believed these commanders could help the US defeat al-Qa'ida and the Taliban. Nearly four years later, many of these same commanders have grown richer and more powerful, with links to organized crime and the narcotics trade, while the Taliban continue to pose a threat. The US, along with senior officials in the UN and in some other governments, has also opposed efforts to investigate past abuses, arguing that to do so would imperil 'stability.' In addition, US forces have replicated some of the same torture techniques, unacknowledged and secret detentions employed by their predecessors, and have thereby undermined efforts to establish in Afghanistan accountable institutions that adhere to the rule of law.[47]

So what remains of the Bush Administration's 'democratizing mission' in the Middle East?[48] Ah yes: the Saudi royal family agreed in 2005 to organize elections in order to designate by (exclusively male) vote half the members of the kingdom's municipal councils – from among duly authorized candidates, including many hardened fundamentalists, who scooped the jackpot. Is there any need to specify that the other half of the municipal council members was not elected by women, but rather appointed by the monarchy? A few months later US Undersecretary of State for Public Diplomacy Karen Hughes, on an official visit to the kingdom, got herself snubbed for questioning, with a keen sense of the priorities for democratic emancipation, the ban on women's right ... to drive.

# Leviathan and the Presidents

Samuel Huntington himself reached a thoroughly Spenglerian conclusion at the end of his much cited, but much less read, book: 'On a worldwide basis Civilization seems in many respects to be yielding to barbarism, generating the image of an unprecedented phenomenon, a global Dark Ages, possibly descending on humanity.'[1]

These global Dark Ages, Huntington explained, seem to confirm:

> the 'sheer chaos' paradigm of world affairs: a global breakdown of law and order, failed states and increasing anarchy in many parts of the world, a global crime wave, transnational mafias and drug cartels, increasing drug addiction in many societies, a general weakening of the family, a decline in trust and social solidarity in many countries, ethnic, religious, and civilizational violence, and rule by the gun prevalent in much of the world.[2]

This is the distressing spectacle of the post-Cold War world, a spectacle that Huntington deplored, in which he saw 'basic elements of Civilization fading away'. The 'sheer chaos' paradigm is nothing more or less than the Hobbesian paradigm of the 'natural condition', or state of nature, which is so much vaunted in works on international relations.[3] Thomas Hobbes conceived of the state of nature as a hypothetical antithesis of Leviathan, his main paradigm and the title of his most famous book. For Hobbes the state of nature consists in a condition of war 'of every man against every man' – not in the sense of a war waged without interruption, but in the sense that 'every man is enemy to every man' and must therefore maintain a constant 'disposition' toward war.[4] This paradigm has often been applied to describe the state of the world before the Second World War, as well as – more dubiously – during the Cold War.

Admittedly, the very concept of a 'cold war' corresponds completely to the definition of the state of war given by the seventeenth-century English philosopher. But the Cold War fundamentally opposed two camps to each other, with each camp being ruled by a superpower. It was not a situation in which, transposing the Hobbesian concept, each state was the enemy of every other and war of all against all prevailed. International society during the Cold War had the peculiarity of being ruled by two Leviathans, in the Hobbesian sense of powers endowed with great force, inspiring fear, and thus guaranteeing peace within and defence of their respective communities. These two rival Leviathans balanced each other out in a global zero-sum game based on what has been quite rightly called a 'balance of terror'. The world was governed by a *duopoly of the legitimate use of physical force*, one might say, paraphrasing Max Weber's famous definition of the modern state. Each superpower had a monopoly inside its own camp on deciding when violence could legitimately be used against another state. The United Nations served for better or worse as the site for managing each side's infringements on the other's turf and the crises that broke out in lands in neither superpower's domain.

The Soviet Leviathan's collapse destabilized this global structure and faced the world with the prospect of a return to a state of nature in international affairs. It was clear, or at least reasonable to suppose, that the US Leviathan would not be able on its own to undertake all the functions of maintaining international order that it had previously carried out in conflictual collaboration with its Soviet counterpart. This made a return to the 'sheer chaos' paradigm all too likely. The openly annexationist invasion of Kuwait by Saddam Hussein's Iraq seemed in some observers' eyes to inaugurate a new international 'state of nature' in which the law of the jungle would prevail. This invasion was ultimately repulsed, thanks to oil interests. But how many other conflicts exploded at various hot spots on the planet, even in Europe, without the only remaining superpower showing any interest in resolving them? The United States itself argued that it could not play world cop all alone, even if it wanted to.

How then could a slide toward chaos, toward a Hobbesian state of war, be averted? This was the main issue raised by the disappearance of the USSR. In other words, how could a monopoly of the legitimate use of physical force be reorganized on a world scale? This was an indispensable precondition for assuring security and order – even bourgeois security and order which, in the last analysis and according to common sense, are preferable to the law of the jungle.

## Two Conceptions of World Order

There were basically two possible ways to reorganize the world after the Cold War, which mirrored the two rival theories – Hobbes's and John Locke's – in seventeenth-century English political philosophy on the birth of the state. These two theories are well known, but often interpreted differently. For this reason we must be clear about the way we define them from the point of view of general political theory before we look at their application to international relations. We need to emphasize that we are taking Hobbes's and Locke's views on the state in general and projecting them onto a world scale, not purporting to give their actual views on relations among states or on England's relationship to the rest of the world.

In Hobbes's conception of Leviathan, sovereign power is established either by force, 'by acquisition', or by political agreement among men, 'by institution'. Both methods are equally founded on 'fear': fear of sovereign power in the first case, and men's fear 'of one another' in the second.[5] So however he may be established, Leviathan rules by means of the fear that he inspires: 'He has the use of so much power and strength conferred on him, that by terror thereof, he is enabled to form the wills of them all.' Each man has 'authorize[d] all his actions' by yielding his individual sovereignty, his 'right of governing myself', to Leviathan.[6]

Contrary to some interpretations, the idea of a contract

('covenant') as the basis of the contractual nature of power is only an artifice in Hobbes's work, a way of concealing the violent character of civil society's subjection. In this way the state always appears to have been legitimized by contract, even when the sovereign power 'by war subdues his enemies to his will, giving them their lives on that condition.'[7] Locke refuted this legitimation of power by conquest, emphasizing rightly that even 'captives, taken in a just and lawful war, and such only, are *subject to a despotical power*, which as it arises not from *compact* so neither is it capable of any, but is the state of war continued.'[8] Michel Foucault generalized this idea of a continuation of a state of civil war – reversing Clausewitz's formula rather than citing Locke – by describing it as essential to all forms of power, of which repression is the basic mechanism.[9]

This is how Foucault criticized the attempt at mystification that he saw at work in Hobbes's conception of sovereignty taking on the form of a contract:

> Sovereignty is, therefore, constituted on the basis of a radical form of will, but it counts for little. That will is bound up with fear, and sovereignty is never shaped from above, or in other words, on the basis of a decision taken by the strong, the victor or the parents. Sovereignty is always shaped from below, and by those who are afraid. Despite the apparent differences between the two great forms of commonwealth (a commonwealth of institution born of mutual agreement, and a commonwealth of acquisition born of a battle), the mechanisms at work are at bottom identical ... It is this discourse of struggle and permanent civil war that Hobbes wards off by making all wars and conquests depend upon a contract, and by thus rescuing the theory of the State.[10]

By contrast with Hobbes's theory, Locke conceived of 'political society' as being founded, starting from a state of nature (which Locke distinguished from a state of war) by freely consented association in order to establish a 'political society' in which the majority rules. (Here we are leaving aside discrimination on the basis of sex or property.) A conception of government flows from this theory that it is subject to the will of the majority. It must act according to rules and laws that ensure the objectives and rights that government was founded to secure, and define the powers of government within the limits of what is necessary to achieve these ends.

> Whosoever therefore out of a state of nature unite into a *community*, must be understood to give up all the power, necessary to the ends for which they unite into society, to the *majority* of the community, unless they expressly agreed in any number greater than the majority ...[11]

> And therefore, whatever form the commonwealth is under, the ruling power ought to govern by *declared* and *received laws*, and not by extemporary dictates and undetermined resolutions. For then mankind will be in a far worse condition, than in the state of nature, if they shall have armed one or a few men with the joint power of a multitude, to force them to obey at pleasure the exorbitant and unlimited decrees of their sudden thoughts, or unrestrained, and till that moment unknown wills without having any measures set down which may guide and justify their actions.[12]

Sovereignty, in the classical sense of absolute and perpetual power in the community, resides in Locke's conception exclusively in the collectivity of associated citizens, who hold a constituent power. '[R]econstructed in this way, the notion of sovereignty acquired a completely different meaning, because it no longer implied for citizens either a structure of subjugation or an unconditional duty to obey.'[13]

*Mutatis mutandis*, we can transpose Hobbes's and Locke's conceptions of political power from the level of relations among individuals to the level of relations among states, from civil society to the society of nations. Each of the two conceptions found its most typical expression in the twentieth century, the first 'American century', in the practices and conceptions of two US presidents. The two were cousins, and even bore the same last name: Theodore and Franklin D. Roosevelt.

After becoming vice president in 1901, the first year of the twentieth century, Theodore Roosevelt took over the presidency following the assassination of William McKinley on 6 September 1901. He continued McKinley's work in the realm of foreign policy, while formulating it more systematically, rather than really innovating. McKinley's presidency (1897–1901) is commonly and rightly considered the decisive moment in the United States' transformation into an imperialist power, although it only pushed its way into the front ranks of international politics during the First World War. Under McKinley the United States projected its 'manifest destiny' onto a world scale, waging war on Spain, extending US rule to Cuba, Puerto Rico, Hawaii and the Philippines, instituting the Open Door policy in China, and taking part in the international repression of the Boxer Rebellion.

Roosevelt had already distinguished himself in Cuba during the Spanish-American War. As president, particularly in US-Latin American relations, he systematized the imperial doctrine he had inherited from McKinley. He thus verified a prediction that G. W. F. Hegel had made in his 1822–31 lectures on the philosophy of history, though in a way that Hegel himself had probably not foreseen: Hegel had seen America as 'the land of the future, where, in the ages that lie before us, the burden of the World's History shall reveal itself – perhaps in a contest between North and South America.'[14]

Theodore Roosevelt's name is associated in the history of US foreign policy with the 'Big Stick', a brutal policy of US hegemony in Latin America. Two of its best-known episodes are the United States' success in getting hold of the Panama Canal Zone and the protectorate it imposed on Cuba through the Platt Amendment. Roosevelt spelled out his doctrine in his annual address to Congress on 6 December 1904. It would become known as the 'Roosevelt Corollary' to the Monroe Doctrine, though in reality it is much more significant than the Monroe Doctrine itself.

This famous speech is the clearest, paradigmatic manifesto in defence of US imperialist interventionism in all the years from

William McKinley to Bill Clinton to George W. Bush. All the interventionist leitmotifs can be heard in it, up to and including humanitarian intervention and war against evil. Speaking in a country with a constitutional tradition based on Locke, Roosevelt laid out a Hobbesian justification for Leviathan's role in the society of nations. He explained in a sense that since there was no chance of establishing a democratic international society, Leviathan had to impose his rule – or rather regional Leviathans had to. The United States took on this role in the Western Hemisphere before being able to extend it to the whole of the 'free world' after the Second World War and then to the whole planet after the Cold War's end.

Roosevelt's speech of 6 December 1904 is so timely that it deserves to be reprinted unabridged. Here we will limit ourselves to citing a few excerpts:

> Within the Nation the individual has now delegated this right [to repair wrongs] to the State, that is, to the representative of all the individuals, and it is a maxim of the law that for every wrong there is a remedy. But in international law we have not advanced by any means as far as we have advanced in municipal law. There is as yet no judicial way of enforcing a right in international law ...
>
> Until some method is devised by which there shall be a degree of international control over offending nations, it would be a wicked thing for the most civilized powers, for those with most sense of international obligations and with keenest and most generous appreciation of the difference between right and wrong, to disarm. If the great civilized nations of the present day should completely disarm, the result would mean an immediate recrudescence of barbarism in one form or another. Under any circumstances a sufficient armament would have to be kept up to serve the purposes of international police; and until international cohesion and the sense of international duties and rights are far more advanced than at present, a nation desirous both of securing respect for

itself and of doing good to others must have a force adequate for the work which it feels is allotted to it as its part of the general world duty ... A great free people owes it to itself and to all mankind not to sink into helplessness before the powers of evil ...

Any country whose people conduct themselves well can count upon our hearty friendship. If a nation shows that it knows how to act with reasonable efficiency and decency in social and political matters, if it keeps order and pays its obligations, it need fear no interference from the United States. Chronic wrongdoing, or an impotence which results in a general loosening of the ties of civilized society, may in America, as elsewhere, ultimately require intervention by some civilized nation, and in the Western Hemisphere the adherence of the United States to the Monroe Doctrine may force the United States, however reluctantly, in flagrant cases of such wrongdoing or impotence, to the exercise of an international police power ... It is a mere truism to say that every nation, whether in America or anywhere else, which desires to maintain its freedom, its independence, must ultimately realize that the right of such independence can not be separated from the responsibility of making good use of it.[15]

Franklin D. Roosevelt took a view contrary to his cousin's. He was profoundly attached to the liberal tradition, in its political dimension going back to Locke, as well as in its Keynesian, reformist socio-economic dimension. Enlightened liberals had come to see these two dimensions of liberalism as one another's necessary complements in a world where social and economic crisis had led to the most frightful dictatorships. The second Roosevelt transposed these two visions onto the level of international relations, in what was and remains the most progressive presidency in the history of the United States in the imperialist era.

Within the framework of US predominance that characterizes this era, the contrast between the two cousins' policies toward Latin

America could not be more striking. Instead of wielding the Big Stick, Franklin Roosevelt practised a 'Good Neighbor Policy' in US relations with the rest of the Americas. He repudiated the open interventionism of the Roosevelt Corollary in 1933, abrogated the Platt Amendment, withdrew the Marines from Haiti, loosened US control over the Dominican Republic, Nicaragua and Panama and reacted with moderation to the nationalization of US agricultural and oil holdings in Mexico, despite pressure from the oil companies for military intervention. A series of Pan-American declarations during his terms of office redefined inter-American relations in a discourse that was more egalitarian and respectful of Latin American countries' sovereignty and independence. At the same time US-Latin American economic relations developed in a way more favourable to Latin American interests.

In his annual address to Congress delivered on 6 January 1941, a sort of manifesto known as the 'Four Freedoms' speech, Roosevelt laid out the guiding principles of his domestic and foreign policy. He listed six principles guiding his domestic policies: 'Equality of opportunity for youth and for others. Jobs for those who can work. Security for those who need it. The ending of special privilege for the few. The preservation of civil liberties for all. The enjoyment of the fruits of scientific progress in a wider and constantly rising standard of living.'

To these he added four guiding principles for US foreign policy, the 'Four Freedoms'. These principles were meant to define US involvement in the Second World War, which Roosevelt was then preparing for:

> In the future days, which we seek to make secure, we look forward to a world founded upon four essential human freedoms.
>
> The first is freedom of speech and expression – everywhere in the world.
>
> The second is freedom of every person to worship God in his own way – everywhere in the world.
>
> The third is freedom from want – which, translated into

world terms, means economic understandings which will secure to every nation a healthy peacetime life for its inhabitants – everywhere in the world.

The fourth is freedom from fear – which, translated into world terms, means a worldwide reduction of armaments to such a point and in such a thorough fashion that no nation will be in a position to commit an act of physical aggression against any neighbor – anywhere in the world.

That is no vision of a distant millennium. It is a definite basis for a kind of world attainable in our own time and generation. That kind of world is the very antithesis of the so-called new order of tyranny which the dictators seek to create with the crash of a bomb.

## Postwar Choices

Franklin Roosevelt's conception of international relations would find its most significant expression in the UN Charter, drafted and adopted immediately after his death in 1945 and largely inspired by the principles he had proclaimed during the war. The Charter's elaboration as the war drew to a close seemed in a sense to fulfill Norbert Elias's astonishingly optimistic prediction in 1939 – a prediction which flowed from his mechanistic and Kantian vision of history, at a time when humanity was plunged into a historically unrivalled Dark Age:

> One can see the first outlines of a worldwide system of tensions composed by alliances and supra-state units of various kinds, the prelude of struggles embracing the whole globe, which are the precondition for a worldwide monopoly of physical force, for a single political institution and thus for the pacification of the earth.[16]

The UN Charter is a contract to which states subscribe by free consent, under which international relations are to be organized according to set rules. It was adopted by the General Assembly, the UN's main legislative body, where decisions are made by majority vote of member states on the equal basis of the principle 'one state, one vote'. The UN Charter aims at ensuring 'that armed force shall not be used, save in the common interest', and that international relations will be governed 'in conformity with the principles of justice and international law' and of 'equal rights and self-determination of peoples'. It also gives high priority to economic and social development, while 'promoting and encouraging respect for human rights and for fundamental freedoms for all without distinction as to race, sex, language, or religion.'

The Charter provided for the creation in case of need of an international armed force, which is supposed to intervene as a last resort to maintain peace within the framework of the Charter's principles and of international law. The Security Council, acting as an executive branch assisted by an international Military Staff Committee, was to control this armed force. Five countries that were part of the victorious coalition in the Second World War secured themselves permanent membership in the Security Council. The Charter gives them an important prerogative, though one consistent with Locke's constitutional principles: the right of veto. The five permanent members of the Security Council have since confirmed their claim to this prerogative by emerging as the world's five main nuclear powers. The country that most forcefully insisted on this veto power – comparable to the veto wielded by an unelected head of state in a monarchical constitution – was actually the Soviet Union. Non-egalitarian by nature, it was and remains the inevitable price to be paid for the UN's existence, and for the possibility of its functioning without falling victim to the first disagreement to come along among the big powers on an issue related to world peace and security.[17]

The UN Charter was never applied and respected as a whole, however, in either letter or spirit. This was due to the worsening tensions between the two global Leviathans – largely a consequence of Harry Truman's accession to the presidency following Roosevelt's death. The UN was reduced in reality to the status of a clearing house for minor transactions between the two superpowers that made up the global duopoly. Their major transactions they generally preferred to negotiate bilaterally, face to face.

The end of the Cold War made it possible – but only *possible* – for the Charter finally to take effect. Many people wanted to believe that a new age was dawning of peace founded on international law. The 'peace dividend' – savings thanks to disarmament, as begun by Mikhail Gorbachev's initiatives – would supposedly make it possible to solve the world's economic problems and create the social conditions for 'the pacification of the earth'.

That would be a way of organizing the post-Cold War world in keeping with Locke and Roosevelt's principles. It would rest on two pillars: the UN on the one hand, with full-fledged application of its Charter, and a kind of global Marshall Plan on the other, on a much greater scale than the original Marshall Plan. Its goal would be wiping out poverty, famine and endemic diseases and promoting development of all countries, in the global 'South' as well as in the 'East'.

This would require the sort of 'Copernican transformation' on the part of US leaders that Georges Bataille called for in 1949, when the world was trading in a World War for the Cold War. They would have had to understand that only US generosity, a gift of its 'excess' in the interest of global development, could have secured the well-being of the world's peoples:

> If a part of wealth (subject to a rough estimate) is doomed to destruction or at least to unproductive use without any possible profit, it is logical, even *inescapable*, to surrender commodities without return. Henceforth ... the possibility of pursuing growth is itself subordinated to giving. The industrial development of the entire world demands of the Americans that they lucidly grasp the necessity, for an economy such as theirs, of having a margin of profitless operations.[18]

> If the threat of war causes the United States to commit the major part of the excess to military manufactures, it will be useless to still speak of a peaceful evolution: in actual fact, war is bound to occur. Mankind will move peacefully toward

a general resolution of its problems only if this threat causes the US to assign a large share of its excess – deliberately and without return – to raising the global standard of living, economic activity thus giving the surplus energy produced an outlet other than war.[19]

The UN's founding and the Marshall Plan gave rise to a first round of illusions after 1945. More recently many naïvely believed George Bush Sr when he announced, on 11 September 1990, that a post-Cold War 'new world order' was at hand:

> ... a new era – freer from the threat of terror, stronger in the pursuit of justice, and more secure in the quest for peace. An era in which the nations of the world, East and West, North and South, can prosper and live in harmony ... A world where the rule of law supplants the rule of the jungle. A world in which nations recognize the shared responsibility for freedom and justice. A world where the strong respect the rights of the weak.[20]

Seldom has a propaganda speech sowed so much mystification. It inaugurated an era of supreme hypocrisy, in which oxymorons like 'humanitarian war' and 'military justice' would be fruitful and multiply. Washington's real choice, made by each successive administration, was Theodore Roosevelt's Hobbesian option, not Franklin Roosevelt's option. Washington chose to extend the Roosevelt Corollary to the whole planet, not to pursue the Four Freedoms. It chose to erect a US Leviathan on fear and hyper-armament, rather than free the world from fear by making a commitment to disarmament.

A few figures shed more light than a long speech ever could. Following the Cold War, US military spending never sank below the floor of 3 percent of GNP and is now on the rise again toward 3.5 percent of GNP. At the same time US spending on official development assistance amounts to barely 0.1 percent of GNP – less than 1 percent of the federal budget, contrasted with the almost 15 percent of the federal budget spent at one time on the Marshall Plan. In other words, US foreign aid amounts to one thirty-fifth of US military spending, and one-seventh of the very modest target set by the UN.[21]

This is the path Washington has chosen, and chosen repeatedly over the years since the Cold War's end: the path of stockpiling means of destruction, the path of greed and miserliness when it comes to foreign aid. This is the path that led from war waged in the name of the UN against Iraq, to war in a NATO framework in Kosovo, and to war against Afghanistan waged by the US Leviathan aided by its faithful British sidekick. And one must be singularly shortsighted not to see that today's global empire is ruled from Washington. When the United States is not acting alone it is using the method the Romans used to expand their empire: in Machiavelli's words, the method of 'forming alliances in which you reserve to yourself the headship, the seat in which the central authority resides, and the right of initiative.'[22]

Far from reversing US policies, the attacks on New York and Washington have only strongly accentuated its Hobbesian, hegemonic and unilateralist post-Cold War course. On this course the US government has arrogated to itself the right to judge the rest of the world and punish whomever it wants, whenever it wants, however it wants. The UN no longer has any function except to legitimate Washington's decisions after the fact – after the exercise of force by and for Washington – and to take on the tasks of stewardship, reconstruction and 'nation-building' in the 'failed states'. In this fashion the United States has been proclaiming to the rest of the world – implicitly at first, but lately more and more explicitly – that the real world is the exact opposite of the fable Bush Senior once told about a 'world where the strong respect the rights of the weak'.

The US message to the world today resembles what the envoys of Athens at the height of its power told the magistrates of the besieged island of Melos, in the famous dialogue imagined by the historian Thucydides: '[W]hat is just is arrived at in human arguments only when the necessity on both sides is equal, and that the powerful exact what they can, while the weak yield what they must.'[23] The Melians responded:

As we think, at any rate, it is expedient (for we are constrained to speak of expediency, since you have in this fashion, ignoring the principle of justice, suggested we speak of what is advantageous) that you should not rule out the principle of the common good ... And this is not less for your interest than for our own, inasmuch as you, if you shall ever meet with a reverse, would not only incur the greatest punishment, but would also become a warning example to others.[24]

In a remarkable little book on the terrorist and non-conventional 'asymmetric threats' threatening the United States, Lieutenant Colonel Kenneth F. McKenzie, Jr, of the US Marine Corps wrote in the year 2000: 'As weak nations, and even nonstate groups, contemplate intimidating or punishing a dominant power on a scale inconceivable 2,500 years ago, we might speak metaphorically of the revenge of the Melians and hear far-distant applause of those islanders.'[25]

Too true.

Perhaps the tragic aura surrounding the whole subject of 'asymmetric threats' explains why those who write about it tend to cite the literature of Greek antiquity. For whatever reason, another book about these same threats targeting the United States' most vulnerable points, written in 1998, referred quite naturally to the myth of Achilles and his famous vulnerable spot, his heel. The book concluded:

In Homer's epic, Achilles was killed only after he had defeated his greatest opponent, Hector, the champion of the Trojans. In a fit of rage, the arrogant Achilles desecrated the body of his slain foe. This angered the god Apollo, who knew of Achilles' hidden vulnerability. Later, as Achilles battled a lesser adversary, Apollo guided an arrow to Achilles' heel, mortally wounding the warrior who had believed he was invincible. The heel was the hero's vulnerability, but hubris proved his greatest weakness.[26]

The arrogant US Achilles, having defeated his Russian foe Hector, continues to grind the vanquished foe into the dust and humiliate him. A much lesser adversary has let fly the arrows that have wounded Achilles seriously at his most vulnerable spot. Flushed with overweening pride, Achilles is lashing out at all his adversaries at once, deluding himself that he can protect his heel by wearing combat boots. His hubris has provoked and will continue to provoke the wrath of Nemesis, goddess of divine vengeance.[27]

# Notes

*Foreword*

1. A. L. Kennedy, 'You can't make an omelette ...', *Sunday Herald* [Glasgow], 23 March 2003.

2. Cited in chapter 1 of this book.

3. 'Transcript of statement made by the Prime Minister Tony Blair', 7 July 2005, 10 Downing Street (web).

4. On Tony Blair's neo-imperial doctrine, see chapter 4.

5. Olivier Roy, 'Why Do They Hate Us? Not Because of Iraq', *New York Times*, 22 July 2005.

6. On bin Laden's motives, see chapters 2 and 3. On the human cost of the embargo imposed on the people of Iraq from 1991 to 2003, see chapter 1.

7. On the relationship between neoliberal 'globalization' and the global resurgence of terrorism, see chapter 3.

8. Excerpts from the al-Qaʿida videotape aired on al-Jazeera TV on 1 September 2005 (translated from Arabic).

9. Ibid. (original in English).

10. Naomi Klein, 'Racism is the terrorists' greatest recruitment tool', *The Guardian*, 13 August 2005 [published as 'Terror's Greatest Recruitment Tool' in *The Nation*, 29 August 2005].

11. The great majority of al-Qaʿida's recruits come directly from Muslim countries, where they have not been exposed directly to oppression of a 'racial' character.

12. Robert Pape's study of the phenomenon of suicide attacks, *Dying to Win: The Strategic Logic of Suicide Terrorism*, New York 2005, bears out entirely what is maintained here. 'Islamic fundamentalism' as such does not explain suicide attacks. (Sri Lanka's Tamil Tigers, a group of 'Marxist-Leninist' origin active in a Hindu population, hold the world record for suicide attacks.) 'Rather, what nearly all suicide terrorist attacks have in common is a specific secular and strategic goal: to compel modern democracies to withdraw military forces from territory that the terrorists consider to be their homeland.' (p. 4) Incidentally, this observation highlights the barbaric uniqueness of the anti-Shiite suicide bombings in Iraq (see chapter 4 of this book).

13. Zbigniew Brzezinski, 'George W. Bush's suicidal statecraft', *International Herald Tribune*, 13 October 2005.

14. Brzezinski, 'A New Age of Solidarity? Don't Count on It,' *Washington Post*, 2 November 2001.

*Introduction*

1. At the same time another attack claimed 58 French lives among the troops of the same multinational force.
2. Ronald Reagan, *An American Life*, New York 1992, p. 466.
3. Caspar Weinberger, 'The Uses of Military Power': speech to the National Press Club, Washington DC, 28 November 1984, reprinted as an appendix to Richard Haas, *Intervention: The Use of American Military Force in the Post Cold War World*, revised edn, Washington DC 1999, p. 203. The five other principles were: 1) no involvement in combat unless the vital interests of the US or its allies are at stake; 2) no involvement without a clear intention of winning and the necessary means to do so; 3) the objectives of the intervention must be clearly defined; 4) constant reassessment of the conditions of involvement and its relationship to vital US interests; and 6) military intervention only as a last resort.
4. Physicians for Human Rights, 'Panama: "Operation Just Cause": The Human Cost of the US Invasion', press release, Boston, 16 December 1990.
5. The Senate and House of Representatives did in fact adopt convergent resolutions in early October 1990 supporting the president's action 'with respect to Iraqi aggression against Kuwait'.
6. This part of the speech is reprinted in George Bush and Brent Scowcroft, *A World Transformed*, New York 1998, p. 370. For the complete text of the speech, see 'President Bush's Address to Congress on the Persian Gulf Situation', *Washington File*, Washington DC: Department of State 1990.
7. Ibid.
8. Ibid.
9. Niccolò Machiavelli, *The Prince*, trans. and ed. Robert M. Adams, New York 1977, chapter 18, pp. 49, 51.
10. Carl von Clausewitz, *On War*, ed. Anatol Rapoport, Harmondsworth 1982, p. 103.

*Chapter One*

1. See Richard Hofstadter, *The Paranoid Style in American Politics and Other Essays*, Cambridge, MA 1996.
2. Stephen Pollard, 'America-Haters Revert to Type', *Wall Street Journal Europe*, 25–26 January 2002. For another sample of the same genre, see the vitriolic article by well-known columnist Charles Krauthammer, 'The Jackals Are Wrong', *Washington Post*, 25 January 2002. Krauthammer's 'howling jackals' are of course US European allies.
3. Salman Rushdie, 'Fighting the Forces of Invisibility', *Washington Post*, 2 October 2001.
4. On the families' recriminations over the amounts offered them ($1.85 million per victim on average), see Elissa Gootman, 'In Last Days for Comment, Victims' Fund Is Under Fire', *New York Times*, 7 January 2002.

The article cites an argument by US Congressman Peter King, who took on the mantle of defender of the victims' families, which if nothing else has the merit of originality: '[G]iven that the World Trade Center was a target partly because it was seen as the embodiment of financial success, those who achieved such success should see that reflected in their awards. "They were the symbols of American capitalism, the symbols of American business, and they were murdered because of what they were," Mr. King said. "Now they shouldn't be deprived of what they're entitled to."' In order not to close on this sordid note, it should be mentioned that a group of 11 September victims' families travelled to Afghanistan to establish a fund for Afghan victims of US bombing – a generous and praiseworthy initiative, even if the projected fund will amount to only $20 million (Lena Sun, 'Sept. 11 Families Ask Aid for Afghans', *Washington Post*, 30 January 2002).

5. Thomas Connor, 'Terror Victims Aren't Entitled to Compensation', *Wall Street Journal*, 6 January 2002.

6. Ibid. 'The families of federal employees received $100,000 approximately each.'

7. George W. Bush, 'Address to a Joint Session of Congress and the American People', White House Office of the Press Secretary, Washington DC, 20 September 2001. Since the United States' attitude toward the Israeli-Palestinian conflict was naturally subject to question after 11 September, Israel's die-hard supporters mobilized quickly to deny any connection. Norman Podhoretz, for example, member of the *Commentary* editorial board, was one of many to use the same kind of argumentation as George W. Bush, as shown in his – racist-inspired – article that appeared in the *Washington Post* the same day as the president's speech to Congress. The article concludes as follows: 'True, the Arabs [*sic*] accuse the US of all manner of horrible crimes. But as someone recently said, what really arouses their enmity is not what America has done wrong but what it has done right. To them the democratic polity and the freedoms that go with it are as corrupting as America's economic system. They want to destroy all this, first in the Middle East itself, and then in as much of the world as they can, so that the way of life they believe is commanded by Allah can rise up again in all its sacred purity from out of the rubble and ashes' (Podhoretz, 'Israel Isn't the Issue', *Wall Street Journal*, 20 September 2001).

8. Dimitri Simes, 'What War Means', *The National Interest*, no. 65-S, Thanksgiving 2001, pp. 35–6. This article includes a cleansing criticism of the Clinton Administration's 'humanitarian' policies. On bin Laden's political motives, see the next chapter.

9. André Glucksmann, *Dostoïevski à Manhattan*, Paris 2002, pp. 15–6. Among other philosophical pearls of the same calibre, here is one more pompous phrase to be found in this same work: 'These kamikazes transform airliners into mini-atom bombs, with the ease of a [Marcel] Duchamp transforming a urinal into a work of art simply by displaying it in an art gallery. In both cases the act is flabbergasting' (p. 34). Less flabbergasting than Glucksmann's analogy, however!

10. Naomi Klein, 'Game Over', *The Nation Online*, 15 September 2001.

11. On the political function of this way of defining an enemy, see Robert Worth, 'A Nation Defined by Its Enemies', *New York Times*, 24 February 2002.

12. Wickert made the remark in an article published in early October 2001 in the magazine *Max*. It brought down solemn reproofs on his head from the German 'political class' and nearly cost him his job. He was obliged to give a humiliating display of public contrition.

13. Dana Milbank, 'Religious Right Finds Its Center in Oval Office', *Washington Post*, 24 December 2001.

14. Elisabeth Bumiller, 'Recent Bushisms Call for a Primer', *New York Times*, 7 January 2002.

15. John Mueller and Karl Mueller, 'Sanctions of Mass Destruction', *Foreign Affairs*, vol. 78, no. 3, May/June 1999, p. 51.

16. Ibid., pp. 51–2. The Muellers added that, in their opinion, the main reason for their compatriots' lack of concern was that the US people considered the sanctions 'an acceptable means of pursuing desirable goals'.

17. Noam Chomsky, 'September 11 and Its Aftermath: Where is the World Heading?' Public Lecture at the Music Academy, Chennai, Madras, India, 10 November 2001 (transcript available on the web). Chomsky had put forward the same idea in earlier speeches, e.g. at the Technology and Culture Forum at MIT (Boston) on 18 October 2001. No one was better equipped to evaluate the relative size of the mass murder on 11 September than Chomsky, who has continually denounced the US government's crimes with all the courage and rectitude of someone carrying out the moral duty of opposing first and foremost his own country's government, the direct oppressor of a great proportion of humanity.

18. André Versaille, 'Retour sur le territoire des Autres', foreword to Gérard Chaliand and Jean Lacouture, *Voyage dans le demi-siècle: Entretiens croisés avec André Versaille*, Brussels 2001, p. 12. The two last questions are in parentheses in the original.

19. See Thomas Friedman, *The Lexus and the Olive Tree: Understanding Globalization*, revised and expanded edn, New York 2000.

20. Friedman, 'Terrorism Game Theory', *New York Times*, 25 September 2001.

21. Mario Vargas Llosa, 'Novelista en New York', *El País*, 25 November 2001, and 'Out of Many, New York', *New York Times*, 11 December 2001.

22. 'To the victims of the attack and their relatives one can offer our deep sympathy, as one does to people whom the US government has victimized. But to accept that somehow an American life is worth more than that of a Rwandan, a Yugoslav, a Vietnamese, a Korean, a Japanese, a Palestinian ... that is unacceptable' (Tariq Ali, 'A Political Solution Is Required', *The Nation Online*, 17 September 2001).

23. Nonetheless, according to a survey carried out by the French marketing and opinion survey institute Sofres for the French-American Foundation, only 10 percent of the French population is 'anti-American'. The group is defined as consisting of people who associate the United States with notions such as 'violence, inequality, racism and imperialism', 'see US foreign policy only as a means for the United States to impose its will on the rest of the world', and 'do

not credit the United States with the desire to maintain peace in the world or assist the development of democracy in countries with emerging economies' (Philippe Méchet, 'En France, l'antiaméricanisme structuré apparaît minoritaire et politique', *Le Monde*, 6–7 January 2001). By a definition like this there are probably at least as many 'anti-Americans' among US citizens as among the French, if not more.

24. Editorial by Jean-Marie Colombani, *Le Monde*, 13 September 2001 (actually published on 12 September). *Le Monde's* zealous solidarity went so far that for several days it published a page taken directly from the *New York Times*, in English – evoking protests from very many readers who do not read English.

25. One of *Newsweek's* editors-in-chief understood the title of *Le Monde's* editorial as follows: 'Yes, the United States had built an international system and it was powerful: Bush Senior's new world order really had come into being after all. This was the meaning of the world's reaction to the September disaster, summed up in the poignant headline in *Le Monde*: "We are all Americans"' (Michael Hirsh, 'America Adrift', *Foreign Affairs*, no. 80, November/December 2001, p. 161).

26. Sigmund Freud, *The Future of an Illusion*, trans. and ed. James Strachey, New York 1961, p. 13.

27. The results of the study are available on the International Rescue Committee's website. See also Karl Vick, 'Death Toll in Congo War May Approach 3 Million', *Washington Post*, 30 April 2001.

28. Barton Gellman, 'An Unequal Calculus of Life and Death', *Washington Post*, 27 December 2000.

29. André Glucksmann cannot be accused of limiting himself to narcissistic compassion. He has devoted himself in a praiseworthy way to the Chechen cause and devoted the best pages of *Dostoïevski à Manhattan* to this subject. Yet even he offers a striking example of 'the mote in one's brother's eye and the beam in one's own'. He only denounces crimes committed by the Russians, Chinese and North Koreans. He does not have a word of sympathy in his book for the victims of NATO or allied countries, such as Kurds and Palestinians. He writes, for instance: '[French serial killer Henri] Landru was fiercely, unanimously condemned for his few dozen killings [actually ten women and one man]. But the North Korean dictator, who has condemned two or three million fellow citizens to death by famine (who knows how many? who cares?), has not been. Nor has the Chinese government, which has allowed AIDS to devastate a vast province for years in order to protect the officials responsible for the disaster' (Glucksmann, *Dostoïevski à Manhattan*, p. 184). But what about the million Iraqis that have already died as a result of the embargo? As for AIDS ...

30. Guy Debord, *The Society of the Spectacle*, trans. Donald Nicholson-Smith, New York 1995, p. 145.

31. Tony Blair, 'Prime Minister's Speech on the Conflict in Afghanistan' to the Welsh Assembly, 30 October 2001.

32. Daniel Schneidermann, 'Effort de guerre', *Le Monde*, editorial in the TV supplement, 4–5 November 2001. Speaking of motes and beams, we should

also mention the diatribe against the Arab TV network al-Jazeera published in the Sunday *New York Times Magazine*, which had the nerve to reproach the Qatari station for (among other things) having 'played and replayed the heart-rending footage of 12-year-old Muhammed al-Durra, who was shot in Gaza and died in his father's arms' (Fouad Ajami, 'What the Muslim World Is Watching', *New York Times Magazine*, 18 November 2001).

33. Shankar Vedantam, 'Discourse Does Not Match Falling Sept. 11 Death Toll', *Washington Post*, 22 November 2001.

*Chapter Two*

1. John Cooley, *Unholy Wars: Afghanistan, America and International Terrorism*, London 1999. A new, expanded edition appeared in 2000; the following citations refer to the page numbers in the first edition.

2. Ibid., pp. 240–1.

3. Karl Marx, 'The Indian Revolt', *New York Daily Tribune*, 16 September 1857, in *Marx and Engels on Britain*, Moscow 1953, pp. 449–50.

4. Ibid., p. 453.

5. 'Many of those bin Laden recruited turned out to be zealous Muslims, like himself, and brave fighters. Some, however, were criminals, like those whom the Tabligh [an Islamic missionary organization] helped to undergo religious training in Pakistan, once they emerged from Algerian or Tunisian prisons' (Cooley, *Unholy Wars*, p. 119).

6. Since the name 'Saudi' refers to the ruling dynasty, I put it in quotation marks whenever it is used to refer to the country or its nationals.

7. 'Hanbalism', named after its founder Ahmad bin Hanbal (780–855), is one of the four doctrines (*madhahib*) recognized by orthodox Sunni Islam. Hanbalism is distinguished by its intolerant dogmatism and its hostility to any innovation in religious matters. Wahhabism, a term that the followers of Muhammad bin Abdel-Wahhab take exception to, is an extreme version of Hanbalism.

8. Only five years later, in 1938, the kingdom's first commercially exploitable oil field was discovered.

9. US forces evacuated the Dhahran base in 1962, after it had become the subject of vehement denunciations by Nasserite Arab nationalists and a major embarrassment for the Saudi regime.

10. Daniel Yergin, *The Prize: The Epic Quest for Oil, Money and Power*, London 1993, p. 427.

11. Ibid., pp. 404–5. During his meeting with Roosevelt, the Saudi monarch also declared, according to the US government account of their conversation: 'You and I want freedom and prosperity for our people and their neighbors after the war. How and by whose hand freedom and prosperity arrive concerns us but little. The English also work and sacrifice to bring freedom and prosperity to the world, but on the condition that it be brought by them and marked "Made in Britain"' (Department of State, *Foreign Relations of the United States, 1945*, 'Near East and Africa', Washington DC: Government Printing Office 1969, p. 8; cited in Joseph McMillan, *US-Saudi Relations: Rebuilding the Strategic*

*Consensus, Strategic Forum* no. 186, Washington DC: Institute for National Strategic Studies, National Defense University, Note 1).

12. 'What We're Fighting For', New York: Institute for American Values, February 2002.

13. Human Rights Watch, *Human Rights in Saudi Arabia: A Deafening Silence*, Washington DC, December 2001, p. 1.

14. On the various aspects of the US-Saudi relationship, see the series of articles by Robert Kaiser and David Ottaway, published under the general title 'Marriage of Convenience: The US-Saudi Alliance', *Washington Post*, 10–12 February 2002.

15. Zbigniew Brzezinski, in transcript of 'The Arming of Saudi Arabia', *Frontline* show #1112, PBS, 16 February 1993.

16. See Alfred Prados, 'Saudi Arabia: Post-War Issues and US Relations', Issue Brief for Congress IB93113, Washington DC: Congressional Research Service, 13 April 2001.

17. 'Gradually this picture began to emerge that we were talking not just about five Awacs planes, but that this was the way to slip in the linchpin to an elaborate electronic communications system that would be the equivalent of the heart of what we have in NATO, for example. It was creating a new theater of war. It was something that the Americans would essentially be able to move into and control instantly. But the key to it was the Saudis were going to pay for it' (Scott Armstrong, in PBS *Frontline* 'The Arming of Saudi Arabia').

18. Zbigniew Brzezinski, 'The Arming of Saudi Arabia'.

19. Lawrence Korb, 'The Arming of Saudi Arabia'.

20. Israel, which has more manoeuvring room and a greater degree of political autonomy from Washington, is often called the fifty-first state, but according to chronological order should really be called the fifty-second. There is, by the way, a certain complementarity in the services that the Saudis and Israelis render the United States. In situations in which Congress or the law interferes with the administration's doing as it likes, for example, Israel deputizes for the United States by providing military services, while the Saudis deputize for the US by providing money (as when they supported the Contras fighting the Sandinista government in Nicaragua).

21. On this subject see Albert Hourani, *Arabic Thought in the Liberal Age, 1798–1939*, Cambridge 1983. The Muslim Brotherhood became Nasser's most intransigent enemy, and tried to assassinate him beginning as early as 1954.

22. Malcolm Kerr, *The Arab Cold War: Gamal 'Abd al-Nasir and His Rivals, 1958–1970*, London 1970.

23. The phrases in quotation marks are taken from Karl Marx, 'Contribution to the Critique of Hegel's Philosophy of Law', in Marx and Engels, *Collected Works*, vol. 3, New York 1975 , pp. 175–6.

24. Marx and Engels, *Manifesto of the Communist Party*, in Marx and Engels, *Collected Works*, vol. 6, New York 1976, p. 494.

25. Gilbert Achcar, 'Onze thèses sur la résurgence actuelle de l'intégrisme islamique', February 1981; English translation as 'Eleven Theses on the Resurgence of Islamic Fundamentalism', in Achcar, *Eastern Cauldron: Islam,*

*Afghanistan, Palestine and Iraq in a Marxist Mirror*, trans. Peter Drucker, New York 2004, pp. 48–59.

26. Jacques Berque has painted a magnificent portrait of Egypt in the first half of the twentieth century in *Egypt: Imperialism and Revolution*, trans. Jean Stewart, New York 1972.

27. The Egyptian Communists ultimately rallied to Nasser's regime, which Moscow described as following 'a non-capitalist path to development'.

28. I entirely agree with the reservations expressed by Maxime Rodinson, notably in *L'Islam: Politique et croyance*, Paris 1993, about the use of this word *Islamism*. 'First of all one risks a confusion with "Islam", since the two words are given as synonyms in many texts and dictionaries' (p. 329). According to Rodinson, the new Orientalists' insistence on using this term is evidence of 'personal strategies for Napoleonic conquest of power or notoriety in the intellectual, and especially the academic, world' (p. 231). The English word fundamentalism (which has come to approximate the meaning of the French *intégrisme*), defined as 'the desire to use religion to solve all social and political problems and, simultaneously, to restore full obedience to dogma and ritual', has the great advantage, unlike 'Islamism', of emphasizing the fact that this way of using religion is not a unique attribute of Islam. Catholic, Protestant, Jewish, Hindu, etc, fundamentalisms also exist, though of course each fundamentalism has its specificities (Rodinson, 'Islam Resurgent?', *Marxism and the Muslim World*, New York 1981, p. 291; originally published as 'Reveil de l'intégrisme musulman?', *Le Monde*, 6–8 December 1978).

29. Gilles Kepel, *Jihad: Expansion et déclin de l'islamisme*, Paris 2000, p. 16. In 2002 Kepel's book was published in English (trans. Anthony F. Roberts, Cambridge, MA) under the title *Jihad: The Trail of Political Islam*. The change of subtitle, downplaying the unconvincing 'decline' thesis, is a telling comment on the fate of the whole book, some key parts of which have been altered by the author without the slightest self-criticism. These are mainly the parts (Introduction and Conclusion) where Kepel tries to give his interpretation of the wealth of factual information that his book includes. As it happens, these are the same parts from which the citations here are taken. I have therefore retained the references to the French edition (which was reprinted unaltered in October 2001 in a pocket edition) with direct translations from the original.

30. Karen DeYoung and Michael Dobbs, 'Bin Laden: Architect of New Global Terrorism – Evolving Movement Combines Old Theology and Modern Technology in Mission Without Borders', *Washington Post*, 16 September 2001.

31. Olivier Roy, *The Failure of Political Islam*, trans. Carol Volk, Cambridge, MA 1994. Roy's work nonetheless quite rightly recognizes that 'we have not heard the last of Islamist protestation', because 'the socioeconomic realities that sustained the Islamist wave are still here and are not going to change: poverty, uprootedness, crises in values and identities, the decay of educational systems, the North–South opposition, the problem of immigrant integration into the host societies' (p. 27). The title of his book was not predicting the decline of 'Islamism' but the failure of its project. Those who never had illusions about

political Islam (unlike Roy himself) expected this failure from the start (as the 1981 article cited above, for example, shows). Roy also makes a distinction between Islamism and neo-fundamentalism, a particularly murky concept that has only added to the general confusion.

32. The man who carried the tidings of the 'end of history' had himself predicted the final triumph of 'liberal democracy' in the Islamic world: 'Indeed, the Islamic world would seem more vulnerable to liberal ideas in the long run than the reverse, since such liberalism has attracted numerous and powerful Muslim adherents over the past century and a half.' Francis Fukuyama, *The End of History and the Last Man*, New York 1992, p. 46.

33. Kepel, *Jihad*, French edn, pp. 548–9. In the English edition (see Note 29), this passage is almost unaltered, except for 'Indonesian President "Gus Dur" Wahid', who has been sacked for incompetence by the Indonesian Assembly and replaced – in real life as in Kepel's book – by 'the new president of Indonesia, Megawati Sukarnoputri' (p. 374). Who will be the next nominees for the role of 'facilitators of Muslim democracy' if there is a second English edition of Kepel's book? We should note in passing Kepel's implicit assumption that a special version of modernity – 'Islamic democracy', combining religion and political and economic modernity 'in an unprecedented way' – is reserved for Muslim countries and for them alone. This assumption, which Olivier Roy shares, is characteristic of what we are calling here the 'new Orientalism'. This new Orientalism is different from the neo-Orientalism that Farhad Khosrokhavar has defined as founded on the assumption that the Islamic world can never be modernized at all ('Du néo-orientalisme de Badie: enjeux et méthodes', *Peuples méditerranéens*, no. 50, January–March 1990, p. 122). The new Orientalism by contrast assumes that the Muslim world can never be *secularized,* so that it will necessarily have to be modernized within the impassable boundaries of the Islamic religion.

34. On Foucault's divagations on Khomeini's Iran, see Rodinson, *L'Islam: politique et croyance*, pp. 301–27, as well as Foucault's own writings in 1978–9 in Michel Foucault, *Dits et écrits II, 1976–1988*, Paris 2001.

35. Fukuyama, 'History Is Still Going Our Way', *Wall Street Journal*, 5 October 2001.

36. José Garçon and Véronique Soulé, 'La quête du martyre s'est propagée – Entretien croisé avec Gilles Kepel et Farhad Khosrokhavar', *Libération*, 19 November 2001. In the English edition of his book, Kepel declares likewise about 11 September: 'In spite of what many hasty commentators contended on its immediate aftermath, the attack on the United States was a desperate symbol of the isolation, fragmentation, and decline of the Islamist movement' (Kepel, *Jihad: The Trail of Political Islam*, p. 375).

37. Ibid, p. 549.

38. See the collective work edited by Ghassan Salamé, *Democracy Without Democrats: The Renewal of Politics in the Muslim World*, London and New York 1994, in which a whole gamut of factors is considered but not the role of the West.

39. Francis Fukuyama, 'Their Target: The Modern World', *Newsweek* special issue,

*Issues 2002*, December 2001–February 2002, p. 62.

40. Gilbert Achcar, 'The Arab World: Absence of Democracy', *Le Monde diplomatique*, English edn, June 1997 [revised translation from French and complete version under original title, 'The Arab Despotic Exception', in Achcar, *Eastern Cauldron*, pp. 69–74]. Similar reflections on the same problem can be found in Lisa Anderson's excellent article, 'Arab Democracy: Dismal Prospects', *World Policy Journal*, vol. 18, no. 3, Fall 2001.

41. On this subject, particularly on the distinction developed by Jeanne Kirkpatrick between 'authoritarian' and 'totalitarian' regimes, see Jeff McMahan, *Reagan and the World: Imperial Policy in the New Cold War*, London 1984, pp. 78–89.

42. Samuel Huntington, *The Clash of Civilizations and the Remaking of World Order*, New York 1998, p. 94.

43. George W. Bush, 'Address to a Joint Session of Congress and the American People'. A *New York Times* report on how White House speechwriters drafted this speech revealed that the word 'totalitarianism' was a substitute for the term 'imperial Communism' used in a previous version. The change was made so as not to offend Russia (D. T. Max, 'The 2,988 Words That Changed a Presidency: An Etymology', *New York Times Magazine*, 7 October 2001). Olivier Roy for his part claims that 'totalitarianism, understood as the absorption of the entirety of the social realm into the political realm, [is] foreign to Islamic culture' – also a dubious assertion (Roy, *The Failure of Political Islam*, p. 10).

44. Fukuyama, *The End of History*, pp. 236–7.

45. Fukuyama, 'Their Target: The Modern World', p. 62.

46. Ibid., p. 63.

47. In this regard it is just as possible, if not easier, to make an analogy between radical Islamic fundamentalism and the far left, as Olivier Roy has done. Roy, however concluded wisely that 'comparisons don't prove anything'. Roy, *The Failure of Political Islam*, pp. 4–7.

48. In an autobiographical interview with the Qatar TV network al-Jazeera in December 1998, bin Laden denied having established direct ties with the United States during the Afghanistan war. He nonetheless justified his objective alliance with the United States by speaking of a temporary convergence of two separate fights against the Soviet Union. He noted speeches he made in the Saudi kingdom in the mid-1980s calling for a boycott of US goods and an attack on US armed forces ('Usama bin Laden yatahaddath' [Osama bin Laden speaks], Arabic transcription on the al-Jazeera website, Doha, 23 September 2001).

Another important source on bin Laden's biography is a document given to the PBS programme *Frontline* by a person described as 'close to bin Laden' who has preferred to remain anonymous. The document confirms bin Laden's claims: 'Since the late seventies he had strong anti-American feeling. He committed himself and [his] family and advised all friends to avoid buying American goods unless it was necessary. He was saying very early in the eighties that the next battle [was] going to be with America.' PBS *Frontline*, 'A Biography of Osama bin Laden', in 'Hunting Bin Laden', show #1713K3, 13 September 2001.

49. Ibid.

50. al-Jazeera, 'Usama bin Laden yatahaddath'. The presence of women in the US armed forces stationed in the Saudi kingdom has a doubly explosive effect. It stirs up male sexist hostility to their presence, as bin Laden's statement shows; at the same time, it is bound to help open Arabian women's eyes to the extreme forms of oppression that they are subjected to. Quite early the presence of US female troops inspired 47 'Saudi' women to the extraordinarily daring act of driving around in their cars for fifteen minutes on 6 November 1990, before suffering the repression visited on them as a result. The presence of US female troops is thus destabilizing, and the US government would undoubtedly have preferred to keep the women out. Thanks to the vigour and vigilance of the US feminist movement, however, the Pentagon was unable to select the troops deployed in the kingdom on the basis of sex. It therefore chose to 'hide' the women by making them wear *abayas* (equivalent to chadors) and forbidding them to go out unaccompanied, drive cars off base or even sit in the front seats of vehicles. A woman pilot has taken Secretary of Defense Donald Rumsfeld to court for sex discrimination and denial of religious freedom, and has already succeeded in having the requirement of wearing *abayas* rescinded. This might be more effective than anything bin Laden's followers can do in contributing to a possible withdrawal of US troops from the kingdom! See Ann Gerhart, 'Saudi Dress Code for Female Troops Revised', *Washington Post*, 23 January 2002.

51. See William B. Quandt, *Saudi Arabia in the 1980s: Foreign Policy, Security and Oil*, Washington DC 1981), pp. 93–7.

52. According to Arab sources cited in PBS *Frontline*, 'A Chronology of His Political Life', in 'Hunting Bin Laden'.

53. 'We realized that these terrifying warriors [the Taliban] were only paper tigers; that the bogeymen holding us back were merely our own phantoms, inhibitions and fears; we realized, in short, that once we had the will we had the means and that the liberation of Afghanistan was within our grasp' (Bernard-Henri Lévy, 'Ce que nous avons appris depuis le 11 septembre', *Le Monde*, 21 December 2001).

54. Barton Gellman, 'The Covert Hunt for bin Laden: Struggles Inside the Government Defined Campaign', *Washington Post*, 20 December 2001.

55. See Bob Woodward and Thomas E. Ricks, 'US Was Foiled Multiple Times in Efforts to Capture bin Laden or Have Him Killed', *Washington Post*, 3 October 2001.

56. For an official definition of 'rendition', see the testimony by former FBI director Louis Freeh to the Senate Judiciary Committee, 'US Government's Response to International Terrorism', *Congressional Statement*, 3 September 1998.

57. Barton Gellman, 'The Covert Hunt for bin Laden'. The recent deportation to Guantánamo in January 2002 of six Arabs alleged to belong to the al-Qa'ida network fits this same pattern. Bosnian local authorities arrested the six and turned them over to the US embassy in contravention of all legal requirements. This caused a general outcry in Bosnia, according to the *Washington Post:* 'The cover of a popular Bosnian magazine last week depicted Uncle Sam urinating

on the country's constitution and the European Human Rights Convention ... Human rights groups that once supported the United States, and in some cases were funded by it, are heatedly complaining' (Daniel Williams, 'Hand-Over of Terrorism Suspects to US Angers Many in Bosnia', *Washington Post*, 31 January 2002).

58. When can we expect the *Protocols of the Elders of Mecca* to roll from the presses? I still remember a caricature that the late, lamented Israel Shahak once indignantly passed around. Published in Israel at the time of the Arab oil boycott that followed the October 1973 Arab-Israeli War, it portrayed the features of a Saudi-looking Arab wearing a keffiyah and holding a globe in his hands with an expression of sheer greed. It was the exact replica of the anti-Semitic caricatures that used to depict 'the Jews' as financial masters of the world.

59. Saudi Prince Bandar bin Sultan, his family's ambassador to Washington, artlessly acknowledged this during a TV interview. Responding to a question about frictions between the FBI and Saudi authorities during the investigation of the Khobar attack, he said, 'I never found the complaints from our allies in the West as damaging politically to Saudi Arabia. I always thought that is an asset. The more Americans complain, or the Europeans, that we are not cooperating on internal matters, the more you give me strength with those – with my people, and with the dissidents – that we are not in the pocket of anybody' (PBS *Frontline*, 'Saudi Time Bomb?', 15 November 2001).

60. In the same interview cited in Note 59, Bandar bin Sultan, who presumably knows what he is talking about, dismissed the estimate of bin Laden's wealth at $300 million as laughable. Bin Sultan estimated bin Laden's fortune as somewhere in the range of $30 to $55 million. In any event, bin Laden's family and the Saudi authorities confiscated most of his assets well before 11 September. The actions attributed to the al-Qa'ida network have not required astronomical sums of money; US investigators estimated the total cost of preparing the 11 September attacks at half a million dollars. What these actions have required above all is very determined people and considerable ingenuity.

61. 'Anti-Islamism' seems well on the way to becoming a new 'socialism of fools', to borrow German socialist August Bebel's description of anti-Semitism.

62. Don Van Natta Jr and Kate Zernike, 'Hijackers' Meticulous Strategy of Brains, Muscle and Practice', *New York Times*, 4 November 2001. We can also cite a remark made on *Frontline* by 'Saudi' anthropologist Mai Yamani – a researcher at London's Royal Institute for International Affairs and the first woman from the kingdom ever to obtain a doctorate from Oxford University – that the 'Saudi' hijackers' patronymics indicate that five of them came from Hijaz tribes and eleven from the province of Asir. 'We know ... that those people still feel at the periphery. Periphery is not only a geographical state, but a whole, you know, politically. They feel isolated and marginalized. Is that linked – the sense of marginalization, exclusion from the center, dissatisfaction, and other sentiments – to their relations and their support for bin Laden? That is one question that should be asked and investigated' (PBS *Frontline*, 'Saudi Time Bomb?').

63. On anomie, see the next chapter.

64. Emile Durkheim, *Suicide: A Study in Sociology,* trans. John A. Spaulding and George Simpson, New York 1966, pp. 241–58.

65. Daniel Pipes, 'God and Mammon: Does Poverty Cause Militant Islam?', *The National Interest*, no. 66, Winter 2001–2. Thus Pipes seems to fail to understand that the 1970s oil boom meant, for many inhabitants of the countries involved, impoverishment due to galloping inflation rather than higher incomes. He seems to have an idyllic view of the social reality of countries like Morocco or Jordan; gives his readers to understand that the Oslo process brought material well-being to the Palestinians in the territories occupied by Israel since 1967; says that Islamic fundamentalism is stronger on the West Bank than in Gaza; and minimizes the rise of fundamentalist currents in Indonesia. The most absurd argument he uses to refute the idea that poverty is a cause of Islamic fundamentalism is his emphasis (p. 18) on the fact that Iranians' increased poverty since 1979 has not increased their support for the Islamic regime that is responsible for it!

66. Terry McDermott, 'A Perfect Soldier', *Los Angeles Times*, 27 January 2002.

*Chapter Three*

1. André Glucksmann, *Dostoïevski à Manhattan*, Paris 2002, p. 82. Glucksmann's clarification of what he means by 'terrorist' is not too reassuring in light of the kind of amalgam he resorts to in the same book: 'In the guise of poor people's rebellions against the IMF, World Bank and "globalization" a particularly bloody mode of elite rotation and renewal is at work, mobilizing the masses ideologically in the name of the race, the nation, the class or God' (p. 31).

2. Ibid., p. 82.

3. Michael Walzer, 'Five Questions About Terrorism', *Dissent*, vol. 49, no. 1, Winter 2002, p. 9. On this issue as in much of his thinking about 'just wars', Walzer is less concerned about any categorical imperative in ethics than about the need to justify whatever Israel is doing.

4. Fyodor Dostoevsky, *The Possessed*, trans. Constance Garnett, New York 1959, p. 470.

5. Osama bin Laden, Interview, May 1998, in PBS *Frontline*, 'Hunting Bin Laden', show #1713K3, 13 September 2001. In the interview that al-Jazeera did several months later with bin Laden, he answered the question 'What does bin Laden want?' by saying, similarly, that he was fighting to liberate the Muslim holy places and for the reign of 'God's Word' on earth ('Usama bin Laden yatahaddath' [Osama bin Laden Speaks], Arabic transcription on the al-Jazeera website, 23 September 2001).

6. Osama bin Laden, message broadcast 7 October 2001 by al-Jazeera, Doha, translated directly from Arabic.

7. William Clinton, 'A National Security Strategy for a New Century', speech delivered at the White House, May 1997.

8. PBS *Frontline*, Osama bin Laden interview, May 1998.

9. Ibid.

10. Al-Jazeera, 'Usama bin Laden yatahaddath'.

11. Ibid.

12. As Jean Baudrillard has seen quite clearly, and dared to put in writing: 'A power's rise to ever greater power increases, logically and inexorably, the desire to destroy it. And it is complicit in its own destruction.' 'L'esprit du terrorisme', *Le Monde*, 3 November 2001. Later in the same article Baudrillard added, interpreting the 11 September bombers' motives with considerable insight: 'The challenge and the duel ... with the enemy power are everything. It has humiliated you, it must be humiliated. And not just exterminated. You must make it lose face.'

13. Ernesto Che Guevara, 'Vietnam and the World Struggle for Freedom (Message to the Tricontinental)' (1967), in *Che Guevara and the Cuban Revolution: Writings and Speeches of Ernesto Che Guevara*, ed. David Deutschmann, Sydney 1987, p. 357.

14. André Malraux, *Man's Estate*, trans. Alastair Macdonald, London 1992, p. 221.

15. Judges 16:27–30, King James Bible.

16. Carl von Clausewitz, *On War*, ed. Anatol Rapoport, Harmondsworth 1982, p. 102.

17. Samuel Huntington, *The Clash of Civilizations and the Remaking of World Order*, New York 1998, p. 41. Of the two bestsellers expressing two different facets of the post-Cold War *Zeitgeist*, Huntington's is clearly superior to Fukuyama's. Despite his simplistic approach and the tendentiousness of many of his theses, Huntington benefits from the great advantage that 'realist' writings have over 'idealist' ones in analysing political reality. Based on considerable primary research, the book overflows with interesting and useful facts. Huntington's relativism about civilizations leads him to critique a certain form of Western ethnocentrism very lucidly and to deconstruct its 'civilizing' discourse. In short, his book projects onto a world scale the same caricatural 'multiculturalism' that he calls on his readers to fight energetically inside the United States.

18. Huntington seems even to have borrowed his book's title from Braudel, who wrote about the Islamic world: 'Islam's economic and social problems are almost all essentially identical, in so far as they arise from the clash between an archaic and traditional Muslim civilization, still largely unchanged, and a modern civilization which challenges it everywhere' (Fernand Braudel, *A History of Civilizations*, trans. Richard Mayne, London 1994, p. 112). Nonetheless, Braudel makes a clear distinction between Arabic-speaking countries – the Arabic language being 'the surest proofs that countries are truly part of the unity of Muslim Civilization' – and countries in other Muslim regions like Black Africa, the Indian subcontinent, Southeast Asia and China, where Islam is mixed with other civilizations. Among the methodological precautions that Braudel considered necessary in studying civilizations, he explicitly rejected 'restricted list of civilizations' (Huntington gives nine of them!) and stressed the need to subdivide what he called (using the English term) 'major civilizations' into even smaller units. Braudel thus not only distinguishes European civilization from American civilizations, whereas Huntington simply lumps together North America, Europe and Australia as 'Western

civilization', but even makes distinctions among various different European civilizations: 'Whatever the label, there is a distinct French civilization, a German one, an Italian, an English one, each with its own characteristics and internal contradictions. To study them all together under the simple heading of Western Civilization seems to me to be too simple an approach' (Fernand Braudel, *On History*, trans. Sarah Matthews, Chicago 1980, p. 201). The way Huntington divides the world up into 'civilizations' is only a projection of his political schemas.

19. Norbert Elias, *The Civilizing Process*, trans. Edmund Jephcott, Cambridge, MA 1994, p. 524.

20. Enzo Traverso, *The Origins of Nazi Violence*, trans. Janet Lloyd, New York 2003, p. 153.

21. Herbert Marcuse, *Eros and Civilization: A Philosophical Inquiry into Freud*, London 1972, p. 81.

22. Karl Marx, 'The Indian Revolt', *New York Daily Tribune*, 16 September 1857, in *Marx and Engels on Britain*, Moscow 1953, p. 452.

23. Molière, *Misanthrope and Other Plays,* trans. John Wood, Harmondsworth 1959, p. 135.

24. Primo Levi, *Survival in Auschwitz and the Reawakening: Two Memoirs,* trans. Stuart Wolf, New York 1986, pp. 88–92.

25. Michel Foucault, *'Society Must Be Defended': Lectures at the Collège de France, 1975–76,* trans. David Macey, London 2003, p. 241. Foucault's comments on 'biopower' in these lectures are more interesting than the few pages on the same subject in *The History of Sexuality* (vol. 1, *An Introduction,* trans. Robert Hurley, London 1978). We see in particular that Foucault writes in *The History of Sexuality* that the old power over life and death 'was replaced by' this new power (p. 138), whereas in *'Society Must Be Defended'* he says more correctly (p. 241): 'And I think that one of the greatest transformations the political right underwent in the nineteenth century was precisely that. I wouldn't say exactly that sovereignty's old right – to take life or let live – was replaced, but it came to be complemented by a new right which does not erase the old right but does penetrate it, permeate it, or rather precisely the opposite right. It is the power to "make" live and "let" die.'

26. Foucault, *'Society Must Be Defended'*, p. 254. English translation slightly altered here ('a basic mechanism of power' instead of 'the basic ...') in light of the French original: *'Il faut défendre la société': Cours au Collège de France, 1976,* Paris 1997, p. 227.

27. 'There is here a *historical continuity* that makes liberal Europe the laboratory of the violence of the twentieth century, and Auschwitz an authentic product of Western civilization.' Traverso, *The Origins of Nazi Violence*, p. 153 (italics in the original).

28. Sigmund Freud, *Civilization and Its Discontents,* trans. James Strachey, New York 1961, pp. 58–9. On the dialectic within Civilization between the two drives see Herbert Marcuse's *Eros and Civilization* (already cited) and Norman Brown's magnificent work, *Life Against Death: The Psychoanalytical Meaning of History*, Hanover, NH 1959.

29. Norbert Elias, *The Civilizing Process*, vol. 1: *The History of Manners*, trans. Edmund Jephcott, New York 1978, p. 192.

30. Carl Schmitt, *Theorie des Partisanen: Zwischenbemerkung zum Begriff des Politischen*, Berlin 1963, p. 95. Schmitt attributed this logic of 'absolute hostility' to both the 'partisan' theorized by Lenin and any possessors of weapons of mass destruction who would ever use them. (He passed over the Nazis' genocidal 'absolute hostility' in silence.) His reflections on Lenin's theory of partisan warfare confused Lenin's 'absolute hostility' to a system with 'absolute hostility' to the people who profit from it: '[Lenin's] absolute enemy was, concretely, the class enemy, the bourgeois, the Western capitalist and his social order in any country where it prevailed' (p. 56). In a sense Schmitt's analysis, including the lack of a national dimension, of 'rootedness', flowing from the global character of the struggle, can be more accurately applied to bin Laden than to Lenin.

31. As one author unexpectedly writes along the same lines: 'The imbalance of resources and the disproportion between the two camps are so overwhelming as to make it impossible to put the terrorist state and its victim on the same level, even when the victim goes too far – since no one is without sin.' He is of course talking only about the clash between Russians and Chechens (Glucksmann, *Dostoïevski à Manhattan*, pp. 177–8).

32. Hannah Arendt, 'Preface to the First Edition', *The Origins of Totalitarianism*, Orlando, FL 1979, p. ix.

33. William Cohen, 'The Global Security Environment', *Report of the Quadrennial Defense Review*, sec. 2, Washington, DC: Department of Defense, May 1997.

34. 'Ramzi Yousef, a follower, killed only six people when he bombed the World Trade Center five weeks after Clinton reached the White House. He had spent $400 on ammonium nitrate and fuel oil to fashion the Feb. 26, 1993, truck bomb. But little-noted testimony of the building's engineers suggested later that, with two or three times the budget, Yousef might have killed tens of thousands in the towers' sudden collapse' (Barton Gellman, 'The Covert Hunt for bin Laden: Struggles Inside the Government Defined Campaign', *Washington Post*, 20 December 2001).

35. As conservative columnist William Safire wrote quite rightly, 'By creating the means to monitor 300 million visits to the US yearly, this administration and a supine opposition are building a system capable of identifying, tracking and spying on 300 million Americans' (Safire, 'The Great Unwatched', *New York Times*, 18 February 2002).

36. Thomas Schelling, *The Strategy of Conflict*, Cambridge, MA 1980, p. 11.

37. Gellman, 'The Covert Hunt for bin Laden'.

38. John Burns, 'On Videotape, Bin Laden Charts a Violent Future', *New York Times*, 9 September 2001.

39. 'The battle of wills therefore comes down to a struggle for freedom of action, each side trying to preserve freedom of action for itself and deny it to the enemy.' André Beaufre, *Introduction to Strategy, with Particular Reference to Problems of Defense, Politics, Economics, and Diplomacy in the Nuclear Age*, trans. R. H. Barry, New York 1965, p. 35.

40. On the central political options debated within the US administration in the 1990s, see Gilbert Achcar, 'Rasputin Plays at Chess: How the West Blundered into a New Cold War', in *Masters of the Universe?: Nato's Balkan Crusade*, ed. Tariq Ali, London 2000.

41. Joint Chiefs of Staff, *Joint Vision 2010*, Washington, DC: Department of Defense 1996, p. 34.

42. Cohen, 'Transforming US Forces for the Future', sec. 7. The notion of US forces' asymmetric advantage is also present in the DOD's *Joint Vision 2010*.

43. Donald Rumsfeld, 'Foreword', in DOD, *Quadrennial Defense Review Report*, 30 September 2001, p. iv.

44. On all these issues, see Gilbert Achcar, 'The Strategic Triad: The United States, Russia and China', *New Left Review*, no. 228 (March–April 1998), reprinted in Ali, ed. *Masters of the Universe*.

45. We must also not forget that Democratic candidate Al Gore largely outdid George W. Bush in the 2000 presidential campaign in promising higher military spending. See Gilbert Achcar, 'The Spirit (and the Budget) of a New Cold War', *The Spokesman*, no. 70 (2001).

46. Rumsfeld, *Quadrennial Defense Review Report*, pp. 18, 21.

47. The Bush Administration is in fact barely exceeding the increase decided on for the coming five years by the Clinton Administration: $120 billion as compared with $112 billion. The new increase, actually the same as what Gore promised during his presidential campaign, is spread out more unevenly because of the $48 billion increase in the first year. The new increase also comes on top of the increase already implemented in the last budget. According to the new plans the 2007 military budget should exceed $450 billion.

48. See, for example, the resounding article that Samuel Huntington wrote on the eve of the Kosovo war: 'The Lonely Superpower', *Foreign Affairs*, vol. 78, no. 2, March/April 1999.

49. For a 'Clintonian' critique of the Bush Administration's unilateralism, see Joseph Nye, 'Seven Tests: Between Concert and Unilateralism', *The National Interest*, no. 66, Winter 2001–2. See also Stewart Patrick, 'Don't Fence Me In: The Perils of Going It Alone', *World Policy Journal*, no. 18, Fall 2001.

50. See Gilbert Achcar, 'Wish Lists of Washington, Moscow and Beijing: A Trio of Soloists', *Le Monde Diplomatique*, English edn, December 2001.

51. See chapter 2.

52. Members of the al-Qa'ida network who want to stay out of Washington's hands thus paradoxically find their safest haven in Europe, even if this means risking a stay in European jails.

53. One Bush Administration guru even wrote on the very day of the attacks, 'We do not yet know whether Osama bin Laden did this, although it appears to have the earmarks of a bin Laden-type operation. But any government that shelters groups capable of this kind of attack, whether or not they can be shown to have been involved in this attack, must pay an exorbitant price.' This startling conception of justice came from Henry Kissinger, whose article's title 'Destroy the Network' (*Washington Post*, 12 September 2001) was inspired by Cato the Elder's 'Delenda est Carthago' ('Carthage must be destroyed').

54. On the subject of Afghan civilians who have died as a direct result of the bombings (without counting 'combatant' deaths, indirect victims or longer-term victims): 'A few researchers have already done some arithmetic, basing their calculations on various news reports. Prof. Marc W. Herold, an economist at the University of New Hampshire, added up at least 3,767 civilian casualties from 7 October to 6 December. Carl Conetta, co-director of the Project on Defense Alternatives, used a more stringent distillation of media accounts and concluded that a better guess would be 1,000 to 1,300 deaths.

    'Whatever the total, the Pentagon would likely continue to insist that it is a bare, if inevitable, minimum. "There is no question but from time to time, innocent people, noncombatants, undoubtedly are killed and that is always unfortunate," Mr Rumsfeld has said repeatedly.' Barry Bearak, 'Unknown Toll in the Fog of War: Civilian Deaths in Afghanistan', *New York Times*, 10 February 2002.

55. Walzer, 'Five Questions About Terrorism', p. 8.

56. The same resolution recognized in its preamble 'the inherent right of individual or collective self-defense in accordance with the Charter.' Only a quite extraordinary conception of law could read this superfluous reminder of a principle written into the UN Charter as an authorization for the United States to wage a unilateral war of reprisals and revenge – not self-defence – against a country accused of harbouring the inspirer of its terrorist attackers. The Security Council proposed to take the necessary measures *itself.* Nor is it an accident that the Charter is cited three times in the resolution. The United States action took place in flagrant violation of the UN Charter.

57. In the absence of the International Criminal Court, which Washington will not countenance because it is inconceivable to the United States that the empire's soldiers could ever be subjected to any jurisdiction other than that of the empire's own courts.

58. A February 2002 manifesto in favour of Bush and Rumsfeld's war showed in this respect its greatest similarity with the casuistical hairsplitting that characterized theological justifications for past imperial wars. Signed by an impressive list of celebrities of the US intellectual establishment – including both Fukuyama and Huntington, the 'evangelical' Richard Mouw, and several religious or secular 'just war' philosophers including (of course) Michael Walzer – the manifesto takes the Augustinian and Thomistic principles of Christian 'just war' doctrine as its starting point. It thus cannot avoid mentioning the principle: 'A just war can only be fought by a legitimate authority with responsibility for public order.' But it takes care to explain first, in a footnote, 'Some people suggest that the "last resort" requirement of just war theory – in essence, the requirement to explore all other reasonable and plausible alternatives to the use of force – is not satisfied until the resort to arms has been approved by a recognized international body, such as the United Nations. This proposition is problematic. First, it is novel; historically, approval by an international body has not been viewed by just war theorists [which ones? going back to the Middle Ages?] as a just cause requirement. Second, it is quite debatable whether an international body such as the UN is in a position to be

the best final judge of when, and under what conditions, a particular resort to arms is justified [is the US government a better "final judge"?]; or whether the attempt by that body to make and enforce such judgments would inevitably compromise its primary mission of humanitarian work [have these honorable intellectuals perhaps confused the UN with the Red Cross?]' (Institute for American Values, 'What We're Fighting For', New York City, February 2002). On the subject of the application of the 'just war' doctrine to the Kosovo war, see Gilbert Achcar, 'Is NATO's Onslaught a "Just War"?', *Monthly Review*, vol. 51, no. 2, June 1999.

59. George W. Bush, 'Address to a Joint Session of Congress and the American People', White House Office of the Press Secretary, Washington DC, 20 September 2001.

60. Donald H. Rumsfeld, interview with Bob Schieffer and Gloria Borger on CBS *Face the Nation*, following DOD Briefing, Washington DC, 23 September 2001. Richard Perle, named by Donald Rumsfeld to head the Pentagon advisory Defense Policy Board, expressed the Bush Administration's unilateralist philosophy even more crudely, in the published transcript of a conference on 4 October 2001, on the impact of the 11 September attacks: 'I do not believe that a coalition is important now in the way that it was before Desert Storm. That coalition – let's be blunt about it – was at least as important in securing 51 votes in the United States Senate as it was in assembling forces capable of dealing with Saddam Hussein's army. Those of us who were involved in that remember very well that the establishment of that coalition was a powerful argument to recalcitrant senators ... I am worried about things that some people are applauding. For example, NATO's support, invoking article 5, troubles me. We do not need it, the political benefits are not worth it, and if it is allowed to establish a precedent – if it is allowed to create the sense that we have to get NATO approval under article 5 before we do whatever we do next – then, on balance, that support will have been more harmful than helpful' ('After September 11: A Conversation', *The National Interest*, no. 65-S, special issue, Thanksgiving 2001, pp. 84–5).

61. Ralph Dannheisser, 'FBI Experts Say Hundreds of Trained al-Qaida Terrorists at Large', *Washington File*, 19 December 2001.

62. 'DOD's Wolfowitz Calls for NATO Military Transformation Agenda', *Washington File*, 4 February 2002.

63. 'If the (orthodox) grammar of "superiority" is compatible with Clinton's project of "shaping the world," the grammar that others are groping for around "asymmetric warfare" (as a dominant or new form of warfare) tends to resonate more with Huntington's paradigm of a clash of civilizations' (Maurice Ronai, 'Asymétrie et clash des civilisations militaires', *Cahiers d'études stratégiques*, no. 25 [1999], p. 36).

64. Zbigniew Brzezinski, *The Grand Chessboard*, New York 1997, p. 40.

65. David Isenberg, 'Welcome to the Postmodern Warfare Era', *IntellectualCapital. com*, vol. 5, no. 40, 30 October 2000.

66. 'Even prosperous American suburbs increasingly are demarcated into separately protected super-rich zones. That phenomenon – which real estate developers

euphemistically call "gated communities" – reflects a disturbing combination of social paranoia and pretentious snobbery. Alas, the approaching US decision to deploy a national missile defense system could transform America itself into an internationally gated community' (Zbigniew Brzezinski, 'Indefensible Decisions', *Washington Post*, 5 May 2000).

67. Fukuyama, 'History Is Still Going Our Way', *Wall Street Journal*, 5 October 2001.

68. On the United States, see Morris Dees and Mark Potok, 'The Future of American Terrorism', *New York Times*, 10 June 2001.

69. Department of State, Bureau of Public Affairs, 'Significant Terrorist Incidents, 1961–2001: A Chronology', Washington DC, 31 October 2001.

70. Richard Falkenrath, Robert Newman and Bradley Thayer, *America's Achilles Heel: Nuclear, Biological and Chemical Terrorism and Covert Attack*, Cambridge, MA 1998, p. 47. Some of the information cited about McVeigh and Aum Shinrikyo has been taken from this source.

71. Gellman, 'The Covert Hunt for bin Laden'.

72. On this subject, see Gilbert Achcar, 'The Spectre of Bioterrorism', *Le Monde Diplomatique*, English edn, July 1998.

73. Foucault, *'Society Must Be Defended'*, p. 254.

74. Pavel Felgenhauer, 'Terrorists One Step Ahead', *Moscow Times*, 9 November 2001.

75. Darshan Johal, editorial, *Habitat Debate, Towards Safer Cities*, vol. 4, no. 1, March 1998.

76. Ibid. Figures cited by Franz Vanderschueren, 'Towards Safer Cities'.

77. Harvard University, *Youth Violence in Urban Communities, Urban Seminar Series on Children's Health and Safety*, Cambridge, MA, May 2000.

78. Figures available on the US Bureau of Justice Statistics website.

79. Vanderschueren, 'Towards Safer Cities'.

80. UNCHS (Nairobi), *The State of the World's Cities Report 2001*, New York 2001, p. 19.

81. Emile Durkheim, *Suicide: A Study in Sociology*, New York 1966, p. 357.

82. Taking inspiration from Durkheim's analysis, we could also study the ways in which different religions – as opposed to 'civilizations' – foster one type of reaction or another to anomie.

83. Durkheim, *Suicide*, pp. 254–5.

84. James Steinberg, cited in Gellman, 'The Covert Hunt for bin Laden'. As director of State Department policy planning, Steinberg had occasion in 1995 to evaluate the extent of this 'dark side', in the framework of a study of threats to the post-Cold War world.

85. Durkheim, *Suicide*, pp. 368, 387.

*Chapter Four*

1. Rudyard Kipling, 'The White Man's Burden', *The Times* [London], 4 February 1899.

2. 'The Hypocrisy of It', editorial in the Chicago Commons bulletin *The Public*, no. 2, 10 June 1899 (reprinted in the anthology '"The White Man's Burden"

and Its Critics', in Jim Zwick, ed., *Anti-Imperialism in the United States, 1898–1935*, at: http://www.boondocksnet.com/ai/).

3. Anatole France, *The White Stone*, trans. Charles Roche, London 1910, pp. 170–1 (the full original text of the 1905 French novel, *Sur la pierre blanche*, is available at: http://gallica.bnf.fr).

4. 'Letter to a Slightly Depressed Antiwar Activist', 14 April 2003, a text published in several languages in several newspapers and periodicals as well as on various websites; reprinted in my book *Eastern Cauldron*, New York 2004, pp. 259–64.

5. On 6 October 2005 a Pentagon spokesperson presented a letter attributed to bin Laden's mentor Ayman al-Zawahiri, advising al-Qa'ida's followers in Iraq to stop resorting to practices like beheadings and bombings of Shiite mosques so as not to alienate the Iraqi people, including Sunnis. (The full text of the letter was made public a few days later.) An audio message attributed to Zarqawi, broadcast on the Internet the next day as if in response to Zawahiri, justified the murder of civilian 'infidels'.

6. Les Roberts *et al.*, 'Mortality before and after the 2003 invasion of Iraq: cluster sample survey', *The Lancet*, vol. 364, no. 9448, 20 November 2004.

7. To the well-known saying that you can't make an omelette without breaking eggs that this argument refers to, Scottish writer A. L. Kennedy has responded in a splendid article: 'You can't make an omelette without breaking eggs – which is to say, because Saddam killed Iraqis and because our illegal bombing of water plants in Desert Storm [1991] made sure that disease killed Iraqis and because our depleted uranium shells left after Desert Storm have meant that radiation killed Iraqis and because our viciously poorly planned sanctions have killed Iraqis, now, to end their suffering, we have to kill Iraqis.' A. L. Kennedy, 'You can't make an omelette ...', *Sunday Herald* [Glasgow], 23 March 2003.

8. 'Hearing of the Senate Armed Services Committee on the United States Military Strategy and Operations in Iraq and the Central Command Area', *Federal News Service*, Washington DC, 29 September 2005.

9. Donald Rumsfeld: 'I've said today that there are a lot more photographs and videos that exist ... If these are released to the public, obviously it's going to make matters worse. That's just a fact. I mean, I looked at them last night, and they're hard to believe.' 'Hearing of the Senate Armed Services Committee on the Treatment of Iraqi Prisoners', *FDCH E-Media Transcripts*, 7 May 2004.

10. *Washington Post*, 'Sworn Statements by Abu Ghraib Detainees': http://www.washingtonpost.com/wp-srv/world/iraq/abughraib/swornstatements042104.html

11. See in particular Seymour Hersh, *Chain of Command: The Road from 9/11 to Abu Ghraib*, New York 2004, and Mark Danner, *Torture and Truth: America, Abu Ghraib, and the War on Terror*, New York 2004.

12. The report indicates that the inhabitants of Fallujah called the torturers at the US base the 'Murderous Maniacs'.

13. Human Rights Watch, 'Leadership Failure: Firsthand Accounts of Torture of Iraqi Detainees by the US Army's 82nd Airborne Division,' 17:3 (G), September 2005, p. 25.

14. Ibid., p. 28.
15. Susan Sontag, 'Regarding the Torture of Others', *New York Times Magazine*, 23 May 2004.
16. Rajiv Chandrasekaran, 'Mistakes Loom Large as Handover Nears', *Washington Post*, 20 June 2004.
17. Michael White, '"Let us reorder this world"', *The Guardian*, 3 October 2001.
18. 'Speech by prime minister, Tony Blair, at the Labour Party conference', 2 October 2001 (speech available on *The Guardian* website).
19. Niall Ferguson, *Empire: The Rise and Demise of the British World Order and the Lessons for Global Power*, London 2002, p. 310.
20. Ibid., p. 311. For a critical analysis of this same neo-imperial doctrine, see Alex Callinicos, *The New Mandarins of American Power*, Cambridge 2003, pp. 34–41.
21. 'They said it first', *The Guardian*, 4 October 2001. On the new apologetics of the imperial epoch in Britain, see Seumas Milne's article, 'Barbarity is the inevitable consequence of foreign rule', *The Guardian*, 27 January 2005.
22. Joseph Chamberlain, 'The True Conception of Empire', Speech at the Annual Royal Colonial Institute Dinner, Hotel Metropole, 31 March 1897 (The Norton Anthology of English Literature: The Victorian Age: Topic 4: Texts and Contexts, at: http://www.wwnorton.com/nael/).
23. See on this subject Adam Hochschild's book *King Leopold's Ghost: A Story of Greed, Terror, and Heroism in Colonial Africa*, New York 1998. On a previously little-known aspect of the British colonial empire's record, see Mike Davis, *Late Victorian Holocausts: El Niño Famines and the Making of the Third World*, London and New York 2001.
24. Léopold II, 'Discours d'ouverture de la Conférence de géographie de Bruxelles', 1876 (cliotexte: justifications du colonialisme, at: http://hypo.ge-dip.etat-ge.ch/www/cliotexte/html/colonisation.colonies.1.html).
25. This is what US Congregationalist minister Josiah Strong wrote in *Our Country*, a book published in 1885 (extracts available on the Internet) which became a bestseller in its time: 'It seems to me that God, with infinite wisdom and skill, is training the Anglo-Saxon race for an hour sure to come in the world's future ... Then will the world enter upon a new stage in its history – *the final competition of races, for which the Anglo-Saxon is being schooled* ... Then this race of unequaled energy, with all the majesty of numbers and the might of wealth behind it – the representative, let us hope, of the largest liberty, the purest Christianity, the highest civilization – having developed peculiarly aggressive traits calculated to impress its institutions upon mankind, will spread itself over the earth.' People don't write like this any more – or not yet?
26. If there was a genocide going on in Iraq, it was the creeping genocide brought about by the embargo imposed on the country from 1991 to 2003, which this book has already discussed in chapter 1. As is well known, the worst genocidal crimes of Saddam Hussein's regime were perpetrated at the time it was waging a war against Iran with backing from Washington and London.
27. See chapter 3.
28. See in particular my previously cited book *Eastern Cauldron*.

29. Besides Jeb Bush, the president's brother and governor of Florida, the three most influential members of the administration that he appointed once he took office in 2001, Dick Cheney, Donald Rumsfeld and Paul Wolfowitz – as it happens the three who were most involved in the Iraq adventure – were among PNAC's twenty-five founders. So were Zalmay Khalilzad, US ambassador (proconsul) in successively Afghanistan and Iraq, and eight other slightly less eminent members of the Bush team and the Pentagon planning team (Elliott Abrams, Eliot A. Cohen, Paula Dobriansky, Aaron Friedberg, Fred C. Ikle, I. Lewis Libby, Peter W. Rodman and Henry S. Rowen).

30. If it regained control of Iran, the US would control 55 percent of the world's oil. These calculations are based on figures supplied by the Organization of Petroleum Exporting Countries, *Annual Statistical Bulletin OPEC 2004*, Vienna 2005.

31. George W. Bush, 'President Discusses the Future of Iraq', Office of the Press Secretary, The White House, 26 February 2003.

32. James Dobbins *et al.*, *America's Role in Nation-Building: From Germany to Iraq*, Santa Monica 2003. We note in passing that Italy is never given as a model, although it probably had more in common with the Iraqi case at its liberation than either Germany or Japan did. In Italy there was a major force in the anti-fascist camp, the Communist Party, which was not under US control and was allied to a rival power – as in Iraq, where Shiite fundamentalist forces were allied with Iran. The US pushed through the Communists' expulsion from the government in 1947. Of course the relationship of forces is not the same in Iraq today.

33. Noah Feldman, *What We Owe Iraq: War and the Ethics of Nation Building*, Princeton, NJ 2004, p. 1.

34. Only of course by postulating, as Huntington does, that democracy is essentially Western can one see any 'paradox' in the fact that peoples can choose democratically to reject Western domination.

35. Thomas Carothers, 'Promoting Democracy and Fighting Terror', *Foreign Affairs*, vol. 82, no. 1, January/February 2003, p. 96. Carothers heads the Democracy and Rule of Law Project of the Carnegie Endowment for International Peace in Washington.

36. Editorial, 'Our Man in Baku', *Washington Post*, 25 January 2004. There is a striking contrast with the pride with which the Bush Administration took credit for its contribution to the Rose Revolution in neighbouring Georgia.

37. 'No WMD in Iraq, source claims', BBC News, 24 September 2003.

38. 'Remarks by the President at the 20th Anniversary of the National Endowment for Democracy, United States Chamber of Commerce', The White House, Washington, 6 November 2003. A few months later, as part of the same effort of 'communication', the Bush Administration launched its stillborn project of the 'Greater Middle East' (see my article, 'Greater Middle East: the US plan', *Le Monde Diplomatique*, English edn, April 2004).

39. English translation published on the Ayatollah's site (www.sistani.org), corrected here on the basis of the original Arabic.

40. Ayatollah Sistani's fatwas, published on his website, prohibit listening to

singing, consider contact with the damp hand of a Hindu or Buddhist (who are not People of the Book) defiling, forbid holding hands before marriage, and ban communication by Internet between men and women, to mention only a few examples.

41. This procedure was ultimately used for the 2005 Iraqi elections, thus vindicating Sistani.

42. The Ayatollah himself used this expression, which was extremely ironic on his part!

43. This great expert in democracy, after having been a member for years of the ruling nomenklatura under the Algerian military dictatorship, was deputy general secretary of the Arab League and then Algerian foreign minister from 1991 to 1993, the years when the military broke off the electoral process and took power directly into its own hands. He also opposed the proposal a few years later to send an international commission of inquiry to investigate the massacres in Algeria.

44. Divide and rule.

45. On the backdrop of the shift that led the Bush Administration to choose Iyad Allawi as its main stalking horse in Iraq, see my article 'Self-Deception and Selective Expertise: Bush's Cakewalk into the Iraq Quagmire' on the *CounterPunch* website, 5 May 2004 (an abridged version of a presentation to a colloquium held on 15–17 April 2004, at the City University of New York (CUNY)).

46. Of course a UN guarantee for the Iraqi Kurds would have evoked a very hostile reaction from the Turkish government, the major regional ally of the United States and the oppressor of the majority of the Kurdish nation.

47. Afghanistan Justice Project, 'Casting Shadows: War Crimes and Crimes against Humanity: 1978–2001', 2005, p. 5.

48. I drew up a general balance sheet of this 'democratizing mission' in 'Arab spring: late and cold', *Le Monde Diplomatique*, English edn, July 2005.

*Conclusion*

1. Samuel Huntington, *The Clash of Civilizations and the Remaking of World Order*, New York 1998, p. 321.

2. Ibid.

3. It is no accident that Robert Kaplan, one of the writers who has tried to demonstrate the validity of this paradigm for the post-Cold War period, uses a citation from *Leviathan* as an epigraph for, and cites Hobbes several times in, his collection of articles on the subject, *The Coming Anarchy: Shattering the Dreams of the Post Cold War*, New York 2000.

4. Thomas Hobbes, *Leviathan*, Harmondsworth 1985, chapter 13, pp. 185–6.

5. Ibid., chapter 20, p. 252.

6. Ibid., chapter 17, p. 227.

7. Ibid., chapter 17, p. 228.

8. John Locke, *The Second Treatise of Government*, §172, in *Two Treatises of Government*, Cambridge 1988, p. 383.

9. Michel Foucault, *'Society Must Be Defended': Lectures at the Collège de France*,

*1975–76,* trans. David Macey, London 2003, p. 15.

10. Ibid., pp. 96, 99. Foucault added, 'and that is of course why the philosophy of right subsequently rewarded Hobbes with the senatorial title of "the father of political philosophy".' This commentary can be compared to that of Jean-Fabien Spitz, a critic of Hobbes in the spirit of Locke. Spitz writes, 'Far from Hobbes's anthropological and political premises being the keystone of modern political philosophy, they are incompatible with the very existence of constitutionalism' (Spitz, *John Locke et les fondements de la liberté moderne,* Paris 2001, p. 334). We can agree with Norberto Bobbio that 'it is hard to find a political thinker who shows more than Hobbes does the essential characteristics of the conservative spirit: political realism, anthropological pessimism, and an anti-conflictualist, inegalitarian conception of society' (Bobbio, 'La théorie politique de Thomas Hobbes', in *L'État et la démocratie internationale,* Brussels 1998, p. 118).

11. Locke, *The Second Treatise of Government,* §99, p. 333 (italics in the original).

12. Locke even described a war of all against all in the Hobbesian sense as preferable on the whole to an *'absolute arbitrary power'* (Ibid., §137, p. 360, italics in the original).

13. Spitz, *John Locke et les Fondements,* p. 290.

14. G. W. F. Hegel, *The Philosophy of History,* trans. J. Sibree, New York 1956), p. 86. The antagonism between the two Americas would 'reveal the key element of the World's History', in the sense that it would foreshadow US relations with the rest of the world; 'Die weltgeschichtliche Wichtigkeit offenbaren soll' (*Vorlesungen über die Philosophie der Weltgeschichte,* Hamburg 1994, vol. 1, p. 209).

15. The text of this speech, and F. D. Roosevelt's 'Four Freedoms' speech following, are easily accessible on the Internet.

16. Norbert Elias, *The Civilizing Process,* trans. Edmund Jephcott, Cambridge, MA 1994, p. 523.

17. Those who demand the abolition of the permanent members' veto and assumption of the UN's executive powers by the General Assembly are not only dreamers but also mistaken from a democratic point of view. They are dreamers, since decisions on international security issues taken by a majority of states on the basis of 'one state, one vote' against the will of the great powers would obviously be subject to a great-power veto by military dissuasion (a situation that incidentally would further privilege the strongest military power, the United States). There is also not the slightest chance of this reform being adopted. It would in any event be mistaken from a democratic point of view: the principle of 'one state, one vote' is not truly democratic, because it puts, for example, a billion Indians and 12,000 Nauruans on the same footing. A truly democratic international organization should have two chambers: a chamber of states on the model of the existing General Assembly and a chamber of peoples elected directly with representation proportional to population. This would resemble the bicameralism existing under the current US Constitution or under the Soviet Constitution of 1923.

18. Georges Bataille, *The Accursed Share: An Essay on General Economy,* vol. 1: *Consumption,* trans. Robert Hurley, New York 1988, pp. 26–7.

19. Ibid., p. 187.
20. George H. W. Bush, Washington DC, 11 September 1996, cited in introduction, Note 6.
21. The United States is last among OECD countries in the percentage of GNP spent on development aid. At the same time the total aid given by the G7, the world's seven richest countries, fell by more than 30 percent in real terms during the last decade of the twentieth century
22. Niccolò Machiavelli, *The Discourses*, trans. Leslie J. Walker and Brian Richardson, Harmondsworth 1970, p. 284. In their bestseller *Empire* (Cambridge, MA 2000), Michael Hardt and Antonio Negri seek to show that the United States today is no longer 'the center of an imperialist project' and that 'Imperialism is over' (pp. xiii–xiv). Their book's success probably has something to do with their method, a hybrid of Hegelianism and postmodernism that takes legal concepts as its 'point of departure' (p. 9) and puts the 'virtual' or 'soft' ('ether') on a par with the material (money and the bomb). Hardt and Negri do concede that the United States still plays a hegemonic role on the level of military force, where it can act alone; but they add immediately that the United States 'prefers to act in collaboration with others under the umbrella of the United Nations' (p. 309). This conclusion, devoid of political perspicacity, serves to prop up their idea that there is no 'new Rome' (p. 347). New York, according to Hardt and Negri, is the centre of global economic power. They fail to see that Washington, the new Rome, is at one and the same time the political and military centre of the real US empire and its decision-making centre on imperial economic policy issues, the seat of the Federal Reserve Board of Governors, the International Monetary Fund and the World Bank.
23. Thucydides, *History of the Peloponnesian War*, trans. C. Foster Smith, vol. 3, Cambridge, MA 1919–23, p. 159.
24. Ibid., pp. 159, 161.
25. Kenneth F. McKenzie, Jr, *The Revenge of the Melians: Asymmetric Threats and the Next QDR*, McNair Paper 62, Washington DC: Institute for National Strategic Studies, National Defense University, 2000, p. x.
26. Richard Falkenrath, Robert Newman and Bradley Thayer, *America's Achilles Heel: Nuclear, Biological and Chemical Terrorism and Covert Attack*, Cambridge, MA 1998), p. 340. 'Hubris' for Falkenrath and his fellow authors refers to US illusions about its own security, rather than to its choices in international politics. Incidentally, the authors should have taken the trouble to verify the source of the myth they used as the guiding metaphor of their work, claimed as being 'in Homer's epic'. Achilles' death from an arrow shot from Paris's bow and guided by Apollo does not appear in the *Iliad*.
27. *Hubris* and *Nemesis* are the subtitles of the two volumes of Ian Kershaw's well-known biography of Hitler.

# Bibliography

Achcar, Gilbert, *Eastern Cauldron: Islam, Afghanistan, Palestine and Iraq in a Marxist Mirror*, trans. Peter Drucker, Monthly Review Press, New York 2004.

—— 'The Strategic Triad: The United States, Russia and China' and 'Rasputin Plays at Chess: How the West Blundered into a New Cold War', in *Masters of the Universe?: Nato's Balkan Crusade*, ed. Tariq Ali, Verso, London 2000.

Arendt, Hannah, *The Origins of Totalitarianism*, Harcourt Brace, Orlando 1979.

Bataille, Georges, *The Accursed Share: An Essay on General Economy*, vol. 1: *Consumption*, trans. Robert Hurley, Zone Books, New York 1988.

Beaufre, André, *Introduction to Strategy, with Particular Reference to Problems of Defense, Politics, Economics, and Diplomacy in the Nuclear Age*, trans. R. H. Barry, Praeger, New York 1965.

Berque, Jacques, *Egypt: Imperialism and Revolution*, trans. Jean Stewart, Praeger, New York 1972.

Bobbio, Norberto, *L'État et la démocratie internationale*, Complexe, Brussels 1998.

Braudel, Fernand, *A History of Civilizations*, trans. Richard Mayne, Penguin, London 1994.

—— *On History*, trans. Sarah Matthews, University of Chicago Press, Chicago 1980.

Brown, Norman, *Life Against Death: The Psychoanalytical Meaning of History*, University Press of New England, Hanover 1959.

Brzezinski, Zbigniew, *The Grand Chessboard*, Basic Books, New York, 1997.

Callinicos, Alex, *The New Mandarins of American Power*, Polity Press, Cambridge 2003.

Clausewitz, Carl von, *On War*, ed. Anatol Rapoport, trans. J. J. Graham, Penguin, Harmondsworth 1982.

Cooley, John, *Unholy Wars: Afghanistan, America and International*

*Terrorism*, Pluto Press, London 1999.

Danner, Mark, *Torture and Truth: America, Abu Ghraib, and the War on Terror*, New York Review Books, New York 2004.

Davis, Mike, *Late Victorian Holocausts: El Niño Famines and the Making of the Third World*, Verso, London and New York 2001.

Debord, Guy, *The Society of the Spectacle*, trans. Donald Nicholson-Smith, Zone Books, New York 1995.

Dobbins, James, *et al.*, *America's Role in Nation-Building: From Germany to Iraq*, Rand, Santa Monica 2003.

Dostoevsky, Fyodor, *The Possessed*, trans. Constance Garnett, Limited Editions Club, New York 1959.

Durkheim, Emile, *Suicide: A Study in Sociology*, trans. John A. Spaulding and George Simpson, Free Press, New York 1966.

Elias, Norbert, *The Civilizing Process*, trans. Edmund Jephcott, Blackwell, Cambridge 1994.

Falkenrath, Richard, Newman, Robert, and Thayer, Bradley, *America's Achilles Heel: Nuclear, Biological and Chemical Terrorism and Covert Attack*, MIT Press, Cambridge, MA 1998.

Feldman, Noah, *What We Owe Iraq: War and the Ethics of Nation Building*, Princeton University Press, Princeton 2004.

Ferguson, Niall, *Empire: The Rise and Demise of the British World Order and the Lessons for Global Power*, Allen Lane, London 2002.

Foucault, Michel, *Dits et écrits II, 1976–1988*, Gallimard, Paris 2001.

—— *The History of Sexuality*, vol. 1, *An Introduction*, trans. Robert Hurley, Penguin, London 1978.

—— *'Society Must Be Defended': Lectures at the Collège de France, 1975–76*, trans. David Macey, Allen Lane, London 2003.

France, Anatole, *The White Stone*, trans. Charles Roche, John Lane, London 1910.

Freud, Sigmund, *Civilization and Its Discontents*, trans. James Strachey, W. W. Norton & Co., New York 1961.

—— *The Future of an Illusion*, trans. and ed. James Strachey, W. W. Norton & Co., New York 1961.

Friedman, Thomas, *The Lexus and the Olive Tree: Understanding Globalization*, revised and expanded edn, Anchor Books, New York 2000.

Fukuyama, Francis, *The End of History and the Last Man*, Avon Books, New York 1992.

Glucksmann, André, *Dostoïevski à Manhattan*, Robert Laffont, Paris 2002.

Guevara, Ernesto Che, *Che Guevara and the Cuban Revolution: Writings and*

*Speeches of Ernesto Che Guevara*, ed. David Deutschmann, Pathfinder/ Pacific and Asia, Sydney 1987.

Haas, Richard, *Intervention: The Use of American Military Force in the Post Cold War World*, revised edn, Brookings Institution, Washington DC 1999.

Hardt, Michael, and Negri, Antonio, *Empire*, Harvard University Press, Cambridge, MA 2000.

Hegel, G. W. F., *The Philosophy of History*, trans. J. Sibree, Dover Publications, New York 1956.

Hersh, Seymour, *Chain of Command: The Road from 9/11 to Abu Ghraib*, New York Review Books, New York 2004.

Hochschild, Adam, *King Leopold's Ghost: A Story of Greed, Terror, and Heroism in Colonial Africa*, Houghton Mifflin, New York 1998.

Hofstadter, Richard, *The Paranoid Style in American Politics and Other Essays*, Harvard University Press, Cambridge, MA 1996.

Hourani, Albert, *Arabic Thought in the Liberal Age, 1798–1939*, Cambridge University Press, Cambridge 1983.

Huntington, Samuel, *The Clash of Civilizations and the Remaking of World Order*, Touchstone, New York 1998.

Kaplan, Robert, *The Coming Anarchy: Shattering the Dreams of the Post Cold War*, Random House, New York 2000.

Kepel, Gilles, *Jihad: The Trail of Political Islam*, trans. Anthony F. Roberts, Harvard University Press, Cambridge, MA 2002.

Kerr, Malcolm, *The Arab Cold War: Gamal 'Abd al-Nasir and His Rivals, 1958–1970*, Oxford University Press, Oxford 1970.

Levi, Primo, *Survival in Auschwitz and the Reawakening: Two Memoirs*, trans. Stuart Wolf, Summit Books, New York 1986.

Locke, John, 'The Second Treatise of Government', in *Two Treatises of Government*, Cambridge University Press, Cambridge 1988.

Machiavelli, Niccolò, *The Discourses*, trans. Leslie J. Walker and Brian Richardson, Penguin, Harmondsworth 1970.

—— *The Prince*, trans. and ed. Robert M. Adams, W. W. Norton & Co., New York 1977.

Malraux, André, *Man's Estate*, trans. Alastair Macdonald, Penguin, London 1992.

Marcuse, Herbert, *Eros and Civilization: A Philosophical Inquiry into Freud*, Abacus, London 1972.

Marx, Karl, 'Contribution to the Critique of Hegel's Philosophy of Law', in Marx and Engels, *Collected Works*, vol. 3, International Publishers, New York 1975.

Marx, Karl, and Engels, Friedrich, *Manifesto of the Communist Party,* in Marx and Engels, *Collected Works,* vol. 6, International Publishers, New York 1976.

—— Marx and Engels on Britain, Foreign Languages Publishing House, Moscow 1953.

Molière, *Misanthrope and Other Plays,* trans. John Wood, Penguin, Harmondsworth 1959.

Pape, Robert, *Dying to Win: The Strategic Logic of Suicide Terrorism,* Random House, New York 2005.

Quandt, William B., *Saudi Arabia in the 1980s: Foreign Policy, Security and Oil,* Brookings Institution, Washington DC 1981.

Reagan, Ronald, *An American Life,* Pocket Books, New York 1992.

Rodinson, Maxime, *L'Islam: politique et croyance,* Fayard, Paris 1993.

—— *Marxism and the Muslim World,* trans. Jean Matthews, Monthly Review Press, New York 1981.

Roy, Olivier, *The Failure of Political Islam,* trans. Carol Volk, Harvard University Press, Cambridge, MA 1994.

Salamé, Ghassan (ed.), *Democracy Without Democrats: The Renewal of Politics in the Muslim World,* I. B. Tauris, London and New York 1994.

Schelling, Thomas, *The Strategy of Conflict,* Harvard University Press, Cambridge, MA 1980.

Schmitt, Carl, *Theorie des Partisanen: Zwischenbemerkung zum Begriff des Politischen,* Duncker & Humblot, Berlin 1963.

Spitz, Jean-Fabien, *John Locke et les fondements de la liberté moderne,* Presses Universitaires de France, Paris 2001.

Thucydides, *History of the Peloponnesian War,* trans. C. Foster Smith, Loeb Classical Library, Harvard University Press, Cambridge, MA 1919–23.

Traverso, Enzo, *The Origins of Nazi Violence,* trans. Janet Lloyd, The New Press, New York 2003.

Yergin, Daniel, *The Prize: The Epic Quest for Oil, Money and Power,* Pocket Books, London 1993.

# Index